Melnikov
An Investigation Through Architectural Models

Melnikov

An Investigation Through Architectural Models

Models created between 2022 and 2024 by students
of the Accademia di architettura di Mendrisio
under the direction of Visiting Professor Pavel Kuznetsov.

Edited by
Pavel Kuznetsov
Marianne Burkhalter
Christian Sumi

Lars Müller Publishers

Context

Discourse

Appendix

The scales featured in the publication are based on various sources.

Introduction

The architecture of the Soviet Union in the 1920s and 1930s made a fundamental contribution to the emergence of modernism in the early twentieth century. An important institution in the young Soviet Union was the avant-garde school VKhUTEMAS, established in 1920. It played a role in modernizing the education of architects, designers and artists in Russia, similar to the role of the Bauhaus in Germany during the same period.

In the search for an architecture and a formal language that not only "accommodated" the new society but also represented its reality (after Hannah Arendt), VKhUTEMAS brought together the most important figures of the modernist movement. The movement maintained close relations with Europe, including Switzerland – see for example El Lissitzky's Wolkenbügel project, which he developed together with Emil Roth and Mart Stam from 1924 to 1925 during his stay in Ticino for tuberculosis treatment.

Konstantin Melnikov is a key figure in this movement. Many of his projects from the 1920s were realized and became icons of modernism. After Stalin's cultural turn in 1932, the avant-garde movement was abruptly interrupted. At the First All-Union Congress of Soviet Architects in 1937, Melnikov came under heavy criticism. He was expected to officially renounce "formalism" (as modernism was generally labeled) and conform to socialist realism, which he refused to do, instead withdrawing into inner emigration. After thirty years of being forgotten, he was rehabilitated and received public recognition just a few years before his death in 1974.

This publication offers a fresh perspective on artistic creation in the former Soviet Union during an era full of hope and responsibility. The models and re-drawings of Melnikov's work presented here were created by students at the Accademia di architettura di Mendrisio under the direction of Visiting Professor Pavel Kuznetsov. They present an investigation and interpretation of available archival material. Executed in a wide range of scales from 1:1 to 1:25,000, they have an immediate, fascinating appearance. Photographs of the models are complemented by surviving sketches from the time, and each project is contextualized in a short text.

Pavel Kuznetsov, Marianne Burkhalter, Christian Sumi
Zurich, Kassel, June 2025

"Saw" Housing Estate General Plan
Competition entries
for the 1st and 2nd rounds
Moscow, 1922–1923

Emanuele Cipolla
Massimo Contini
Scale 1:500

Konstantin Melnikov's entry into the architectural scene coincided with the post–Russian Civil War revival of professional life, marked by the first competitions for workers' housing in an industrial suburb of Moscow.

His proposal for this housing estate was nicknamed "the Saw" because of its distinctive layout of internal streets of family duplexes, each with direct garden access, that resembled saw teeth. Two years later, he would reinterpret the "saw" motif in kiosks for the New Sukharev Market.

The design stood out for its modular forms that used standardized units and solutions that ensured privacy for all types of households. Four housing blocks for singles were connected by an elevated gallery to a main building containing a communal canteen and collective recreational spaces. Invited for the second round of the competition, Melnikov introduced another typology: a circular house-commune with a dynamic, propeller-like plan. While preserving private rooms and entrances, it emphasized collective life and shared space.

General plan for the 1st (top) and 2nd (bottom) round of the competition

МАХОРКА
ВСЕРОСС
МАХОРОЧ

Makhorka Pavilion
Moscow, 1923

Makhorka Pavilion
Moscow, 1923

Simone Mirabella
Nora Soldati
Scale 1:33

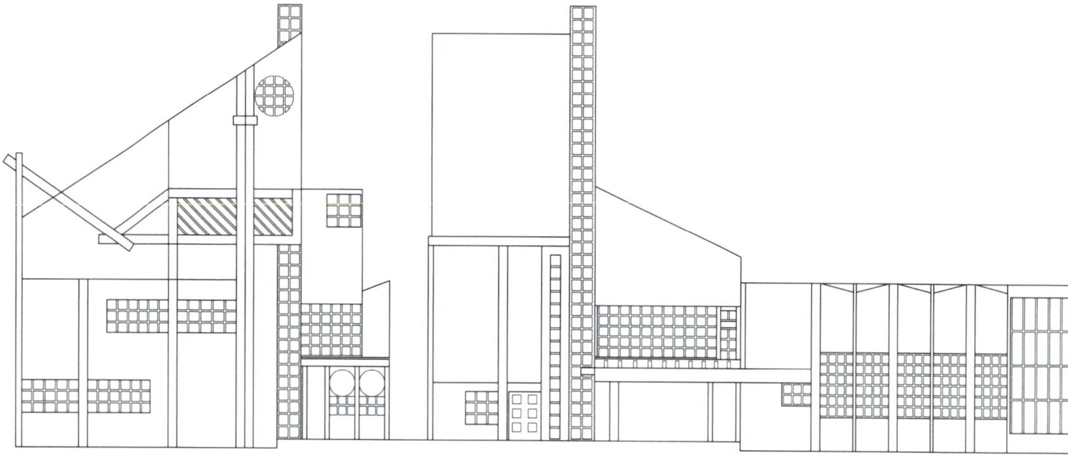

Elevations

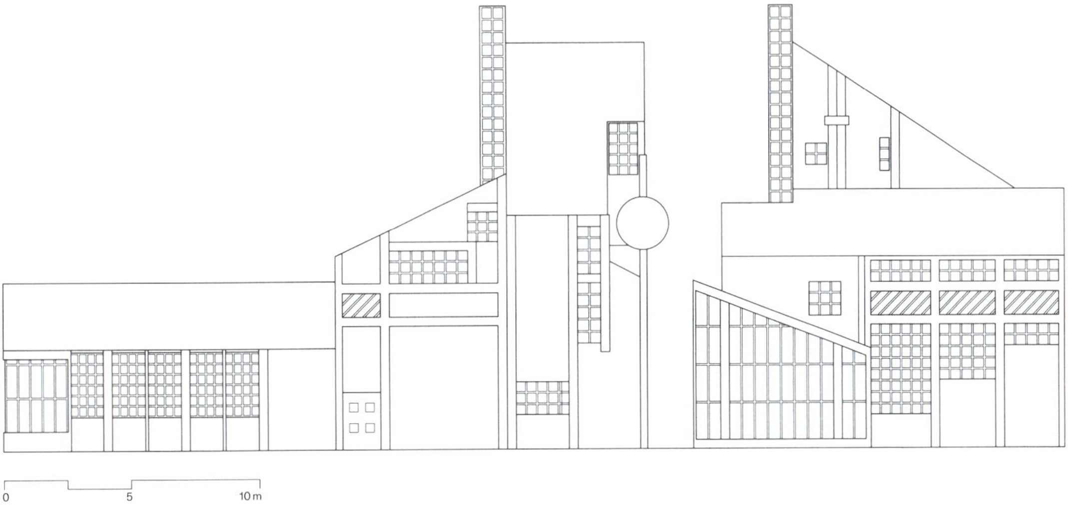

This low-budget wooden pavilion, designed as a mini tobacco factory with live exhibits for the First All-Russian Agricultural Exhibition, was Melnikov's first realized project. Defying the client's expectations, he replaced the standard horizontal layout with a vertical flow that shaped the building's form. Makhorka consists of three single-slope volumes merged into one. Visitors were a part of the immersive show, following the tobacco processing stages – cultivation, drying, fermentation, sifting, shredding, pressing and packaging – as they ascended through the three levels. The route ended with a remarkable exit down the spiral cantilevered staircase. The broken path created shifting perspectives, while a solid protruding volume with supergraphics resembling a pack of *makhorka* tobacco made the pavilion an example of *architecture parlante*.

Sarcophagus for Lenin's Body
Unbuilt version
Moscow, 1924

Vittoria Betti
Andrea Vailati
Scale 1:5

After the death of Communist leader Vladimir Lenin in January 1924, Melnikov was suddenly drawn into a top-secret, career-defining commission. The Soviet leadership had resolved to preserve Lenin's body through mummification and enshrine it in a permanent public display within the Mausoleum. The State Funeral Commission was renamed the Immortalization Commission. In February, Melnikov easily won the closed competition and until July he worked intensively on multiple versions of the sarcophagus, with at least six proposals submitted for approval. This was a commission with no margin for error, closely supervised by the secret police.

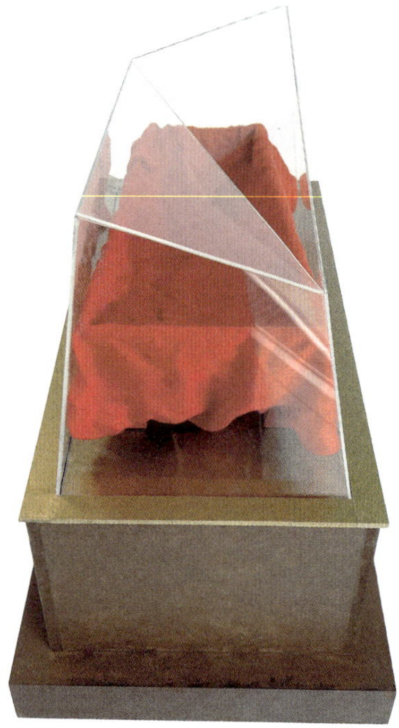

The most striking design featured Melnikov's favored diagonal, splitting the glass into twin crystal forms and suggesting not death but eternal sleep. Ultimately, another version – a simplified trapezoidal pyramid with a four-sloped glass cover – was implemented, later to be dismantled at the end of World War II. The sarcophagus project launched the young architect's meteoric rise and later served as a shield during hard times in his life.

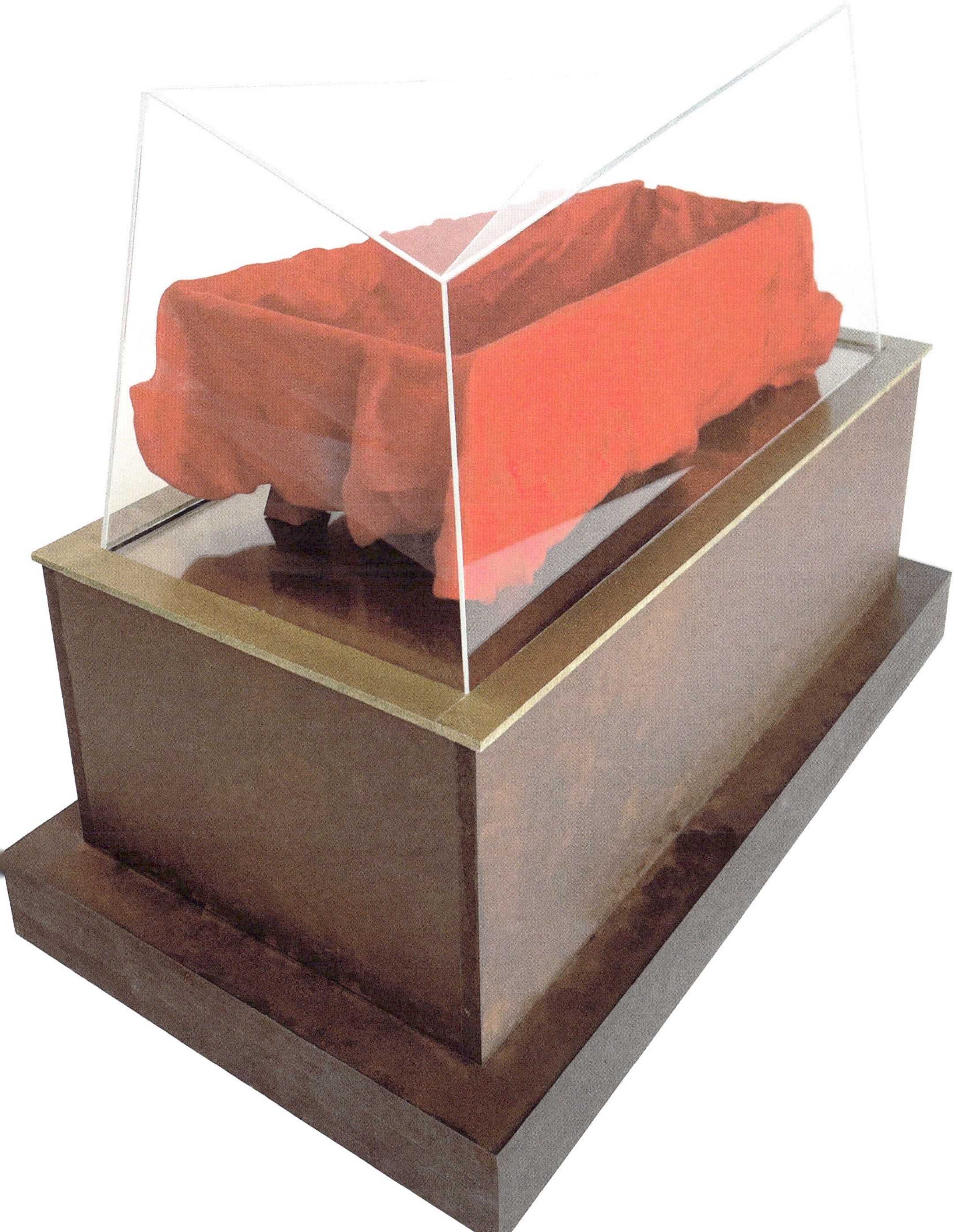

Leningrad Pravda Newspaper
Competition entry
Moscow, 1924

Marten Viohl
Till Zerkaulen
Scale 1:50

This tower, located on a small 6-by-6-meter plot, is a pioneering work of kinetic architecture – an echo of Tatlin Tower (1919–1920) and a predecessor to the Villa Girasole (Angelo Invernizzi, 1929–1935). Four of its six floors could rotate around a central core (staircase and elevator), creating an "endless extravaganza" of facades. According to Melnikov, each floor could be moved manually by the newspaper staff for one-fifth of a full circle. A curving staircase ran along the outside of each rotating volume, allowing public access to terraces above and below. Zigzagging I-beams encircling the glass facades served both aesthetic and structural roles. The competition brief included a newsstand, reading room and editorial offices, but the author reimagined the building as a dynamic tool of propaganda and interaction with the city.

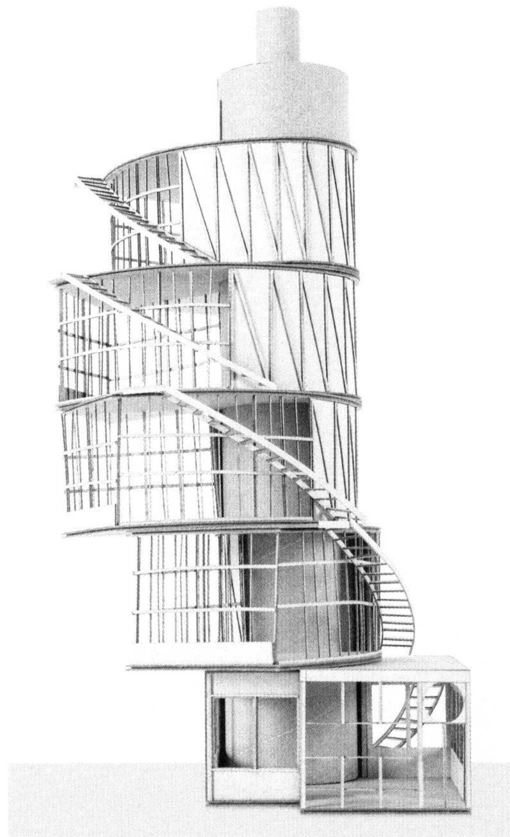

New Sukharev Market
General plan
Moscow, 1924–1926

Marina Bruno
Federico Cigolini
Scale 1:200

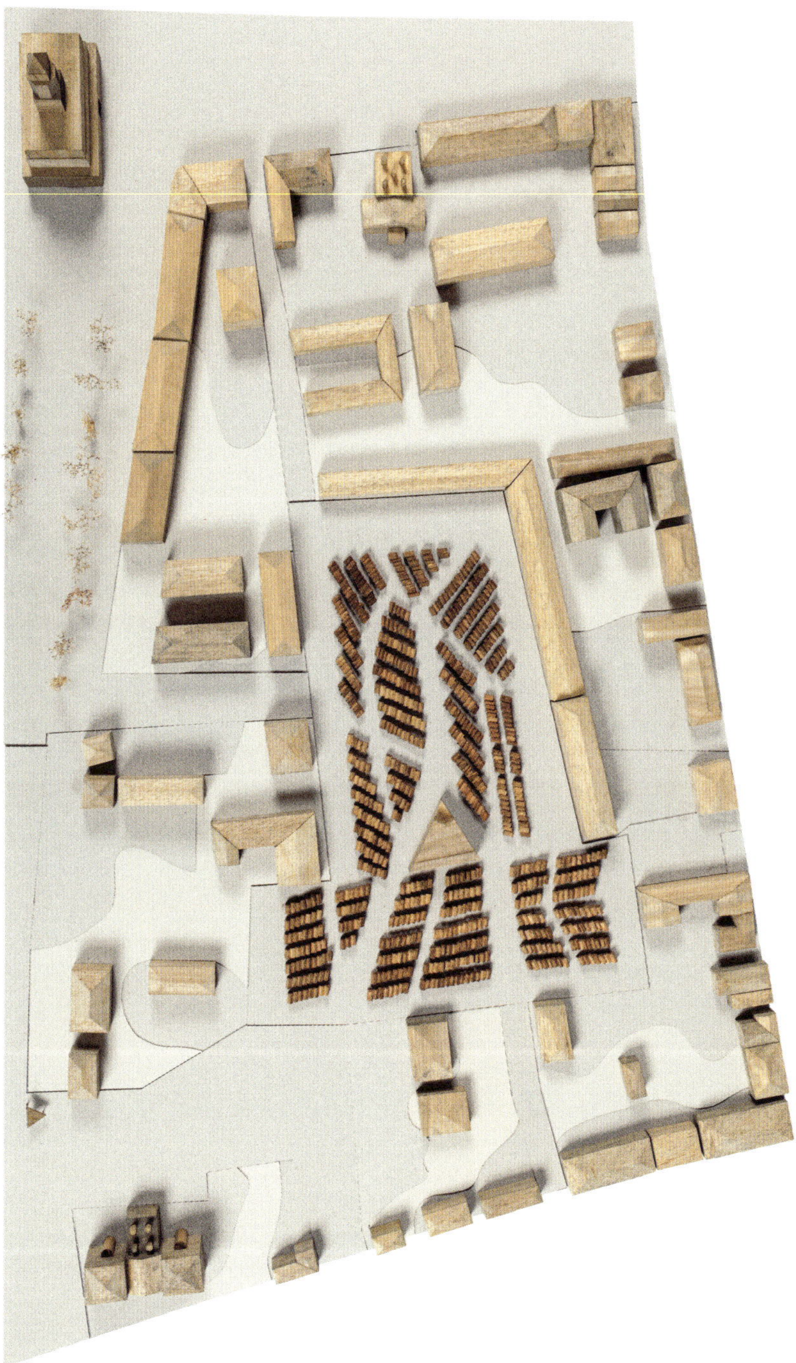

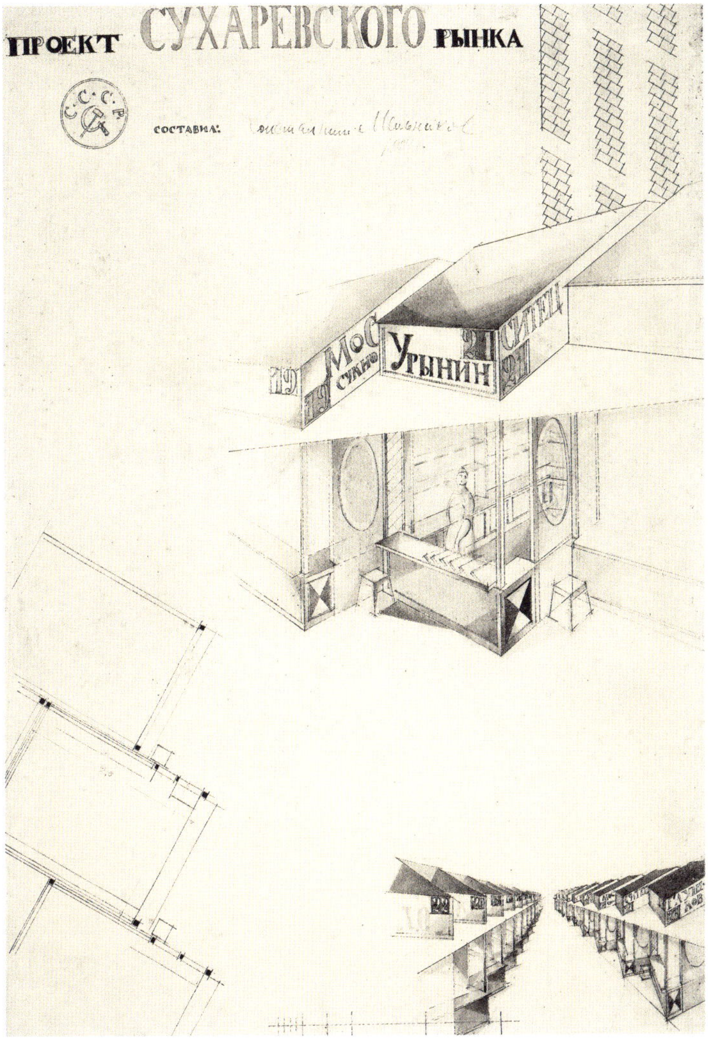

Elevations and plan of the kiosks and trade rows

Initial version of the general plan: "Centralization scheme with the shortest distances from entrances according to the system of Prof. K.S. Melnikov"

Designed and built from 1924 to 1926, the new retail market introduced a novel "city within a city" concept, integrating the area into Moscow's growing urban fabric. Based on a radial master plan, it broke from traditional market layouts with angled rows of over 1,000 kiosks, forming a geometric, saw-like pattern. This allowed buyers to view goods along entire aisles and move freely. The elliptical central square created an interior-like public space, anchored by the office and restaurant building – a visual and compositional focal point. Each kiosk had a number and a two-tone color scheme corresponding to its specific group and subgroup of goods. Melnikov's color scheme transformed the market into a "sea of architectural painting."

New Sukharev Market
Office Building and Restaurant
Moscow, 1924–1926

New Sukharev Market
Office Building and Restaurant
Moscow, 1924–1926

Filip Pawłowski
Dominika Wąsik
Scale 1:75

Flea market in front of the New Sukharev Market, 1929. Melnikov's building is visible in the background

This office and restaurant building was Melnikov's first permanent structure. Initially conceived as two interlocking circular halves, the plan soon evolved into a triangular form responding to the acute angles of the market layout. The white triangle rising above the sea of stalls was the market's functional and compositional center. Its geometry emphasized dynamism and centripetal flow. Melnikov applied his signature techniques here: an unusual form of plan, simple geometric shapes, rhythmic vertical elements, a color scheme with contrasts. Three distinct staircases – two of which led to a rooftop restaurant – separated flows between the restaurant and offices. Visual axes aligned with historic landmarks and churches, while the sharp form of the plan embodied what the author called a "full-bodied slenderness of triangle."[1]

1 Konstantin Melnikov, "Architecture of My Life," manuscript, Melnikov House archive, inv. 1060, (1967).

First floor plan

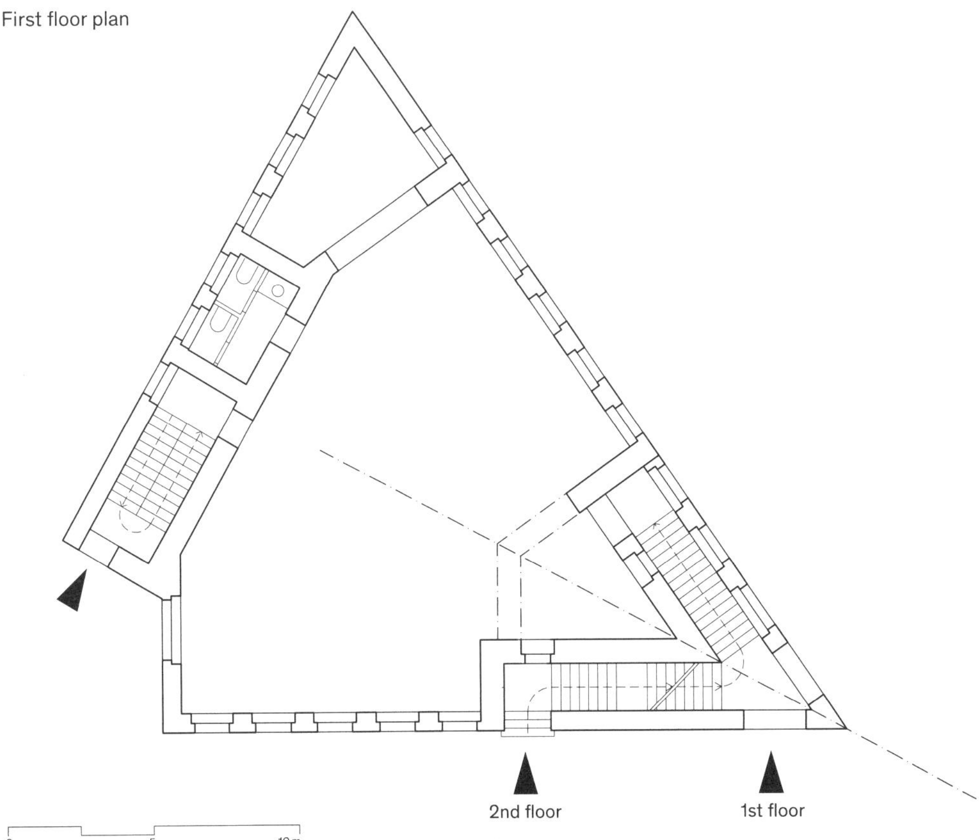

USSR Pavilion for the International Exposition
Paris, 1924–1925

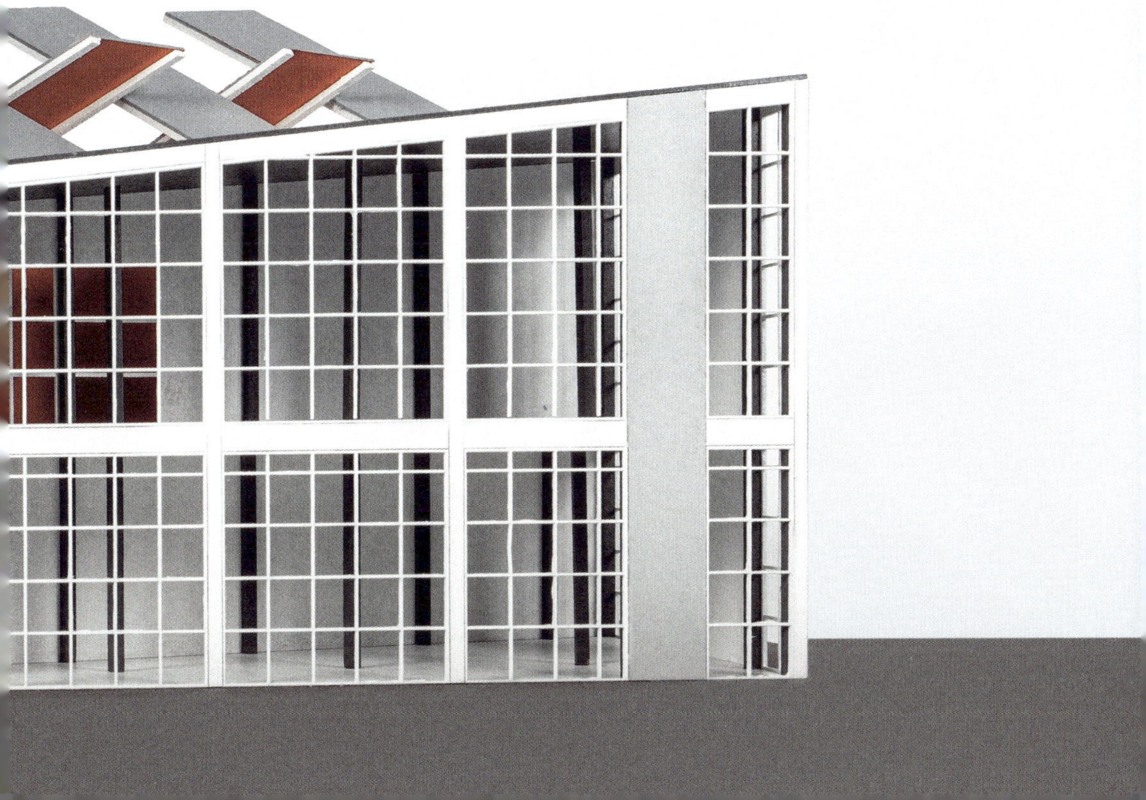

USSR Pavilion for the International Exposition Paris, 1924–1925

Pierre Edmond Courvoisier
Piotr Kadłubowski
Scale 1:50

A pivotal work in Melnikov's career, this pavilion – like Le Corbusier's neighboring L'Esprit Nouveau – stood in stark contrast to the predominantly palace-like European pavilions. Built quickly with lightweight wood and glass on a site with no foundation, it merged modern techniques with vernacular tradition. A dramatic open staircase to the mezzanine cut the building diagonally into two sharp triangular volumes, bringing dynamic tension to its otherwise static rectangular layout. Nine crossed panels above the staircase sheltered visitors from sun and rain. One entrance bore Antoine Pevsner's iron hammer and sickle; the other, the letters "USSR" atop a lattice mast. Alexander Rodchenko's red, gray and white color scheme reinforced a vision of Soviet modernity in motion.

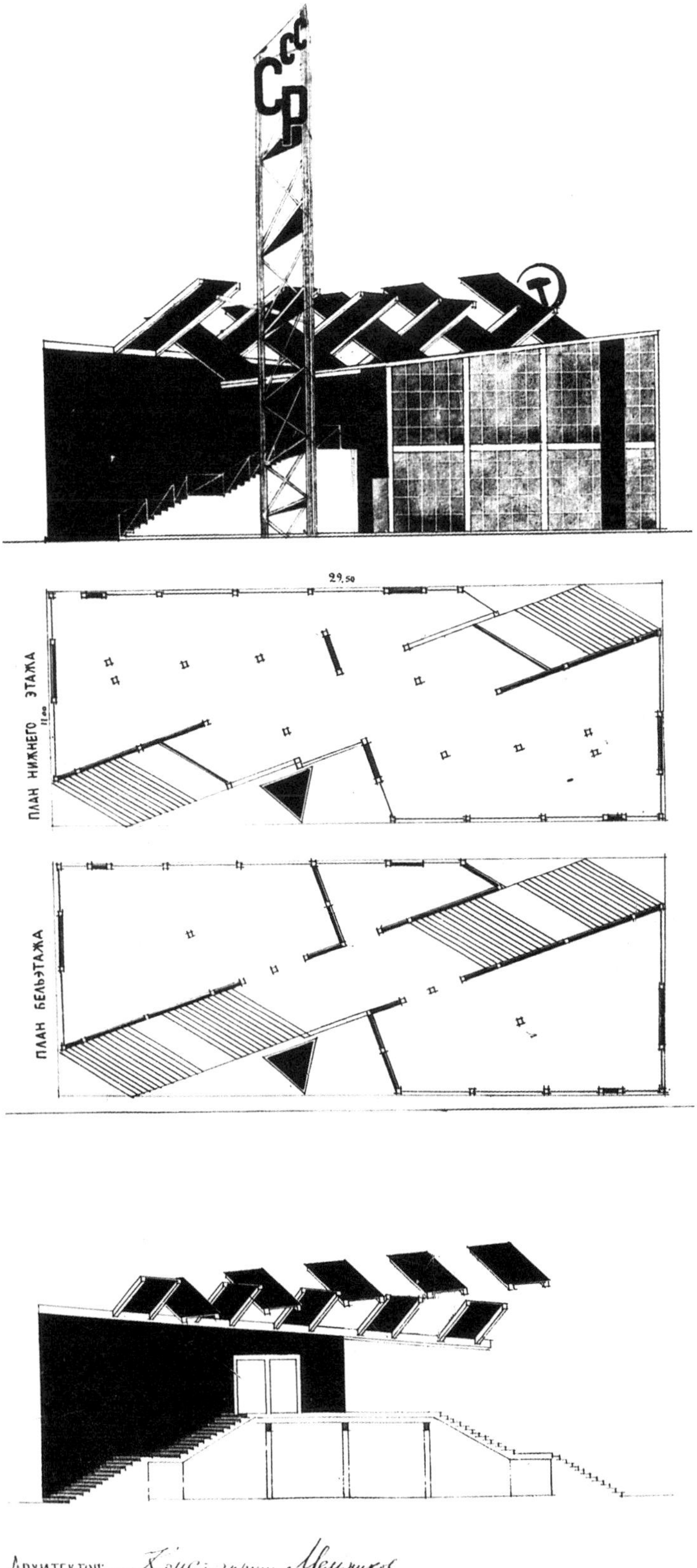

Elevation, floor plans and section

USSR Trade Sector Kiosks
for the International Exposition
Paris, 1925

Pierre Edmond Courvoisier
Piotr Kadłubowski
Scale 1:50

USSR Trade Sector Kiosks for the International Exposition Paris, 1925

Rui Chen
Chia-I Cheng
Scale 1:50

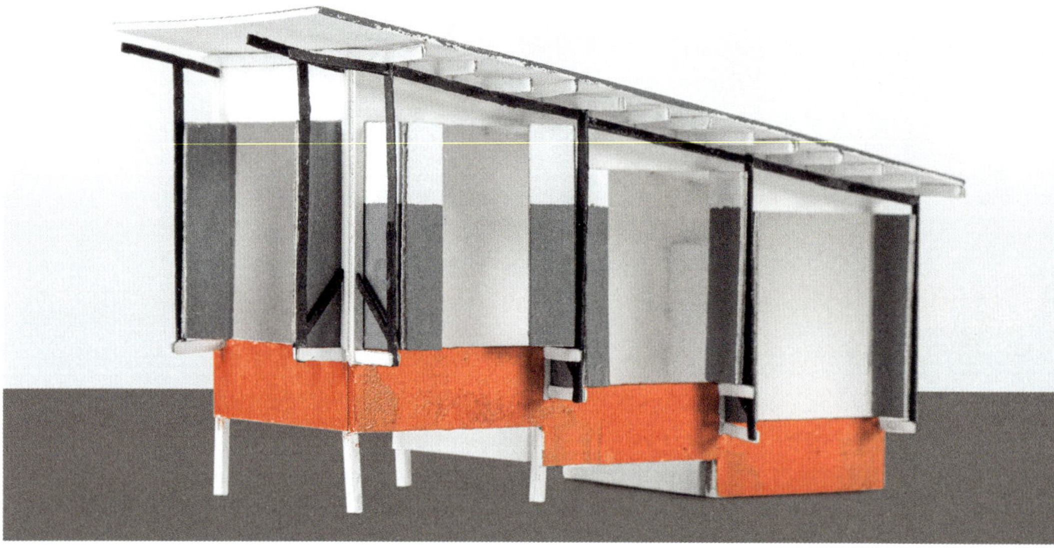

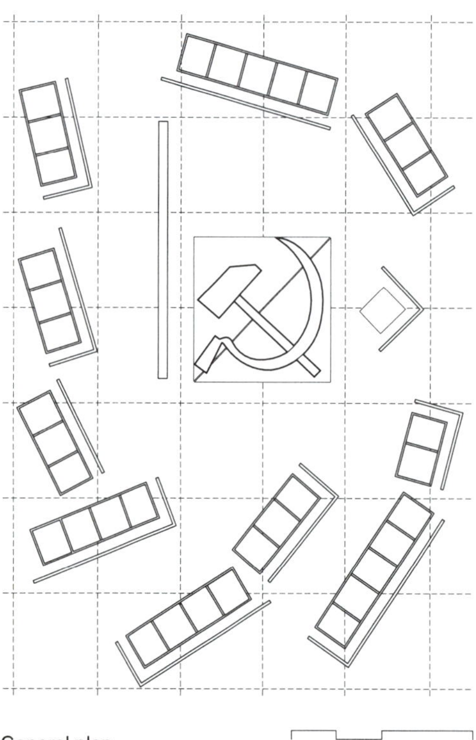

General plan

Melnikov received this last-minute commission, meant to showcase the revival of the Soviet economy, after a quick informal competition held in Paris itself. Installed among trees planted in a strict checkerboard pattern on the Esplanade des Invalides, the kiosks – modular units combined in chains of two to five – visually expressed the logic of standardization and seriality. In contrast, their swirl-like placement defied the trees' rigid grid, introducing spatial dynamism and instability. "The curve contrasts the chessboard order," the author noted on the general plan. Inspired by motion, Melnikov often used vortex and propeller shapes in his site designs. Inside the kiosks, counters and windows at varying heights reflected his belief that architecture, like human interaction, is perceived differently depending on the viewer's eye level.

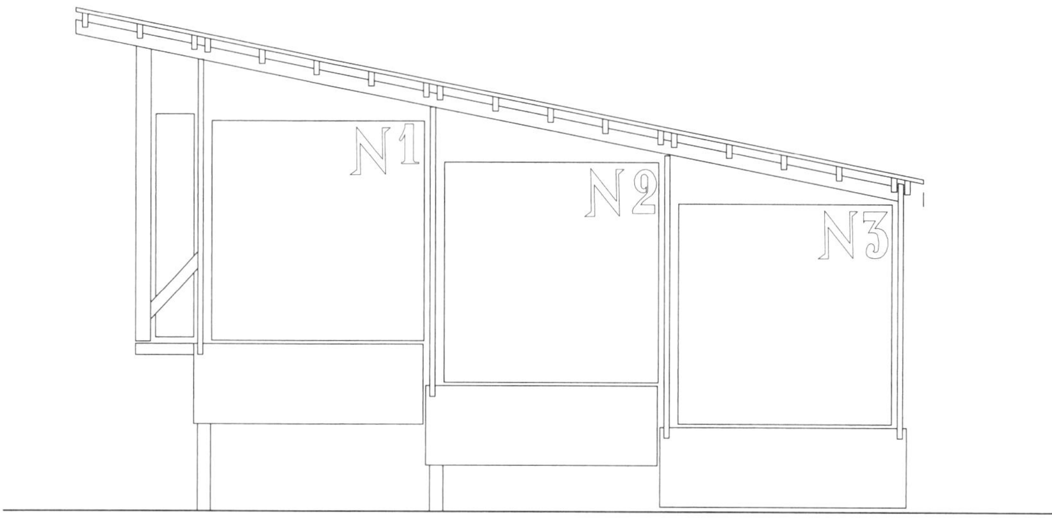

Elevation of the kiosk facade

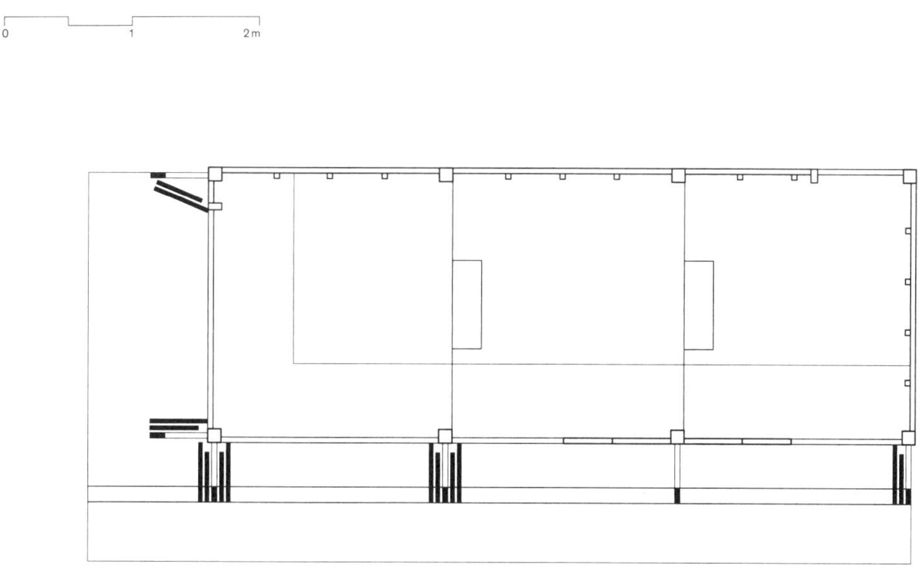

Floor plan

Garage over Seine Bridge for 1,000 Cars
Unbuilt
Paris, 1925

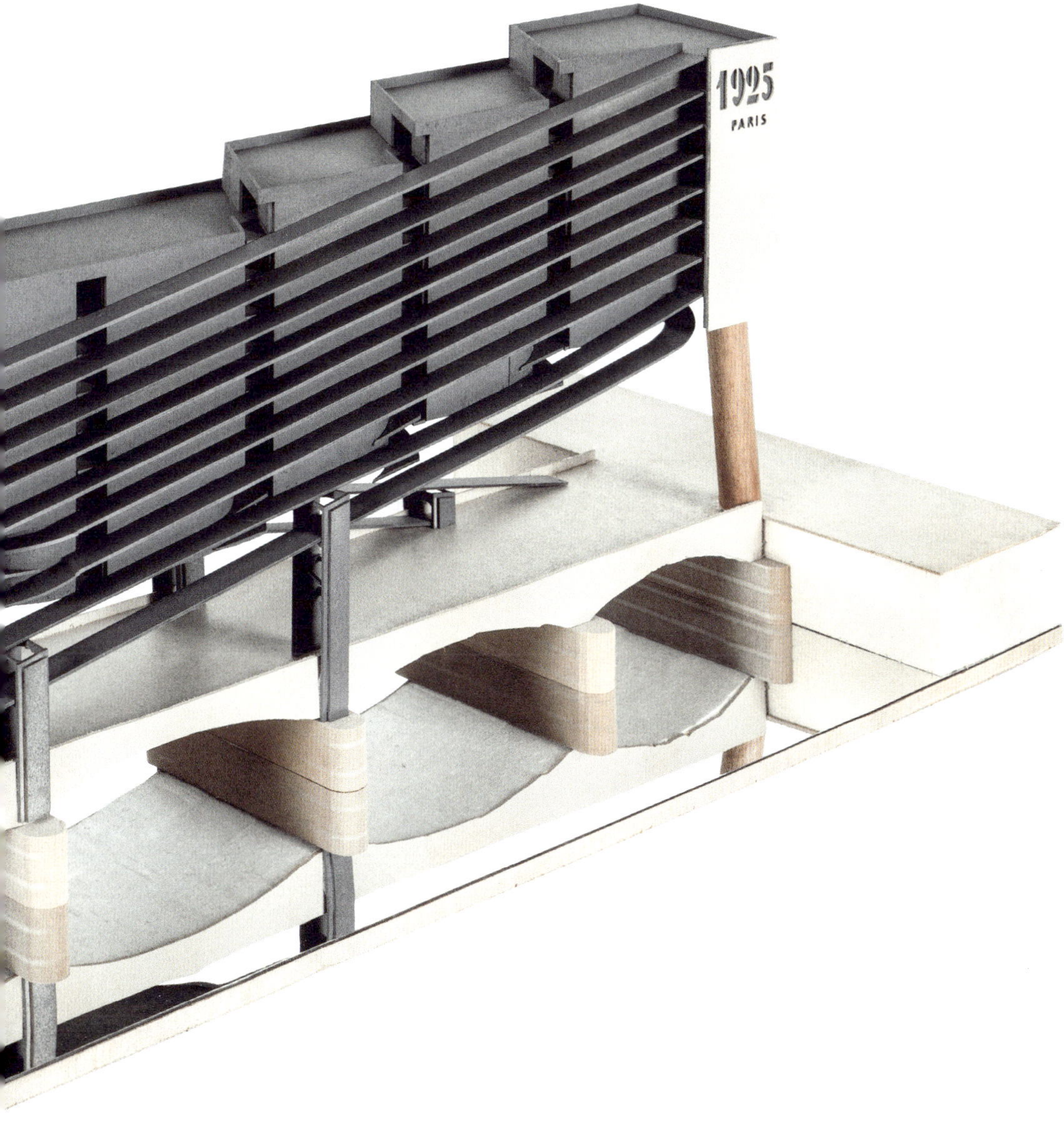
1925
PARIS

Garage over Seine Bridge for 1,000 Cars
Unbuilt
Paris, 1925

Niccolò Pasti
Mauro Cecchetti
Scale 1:200

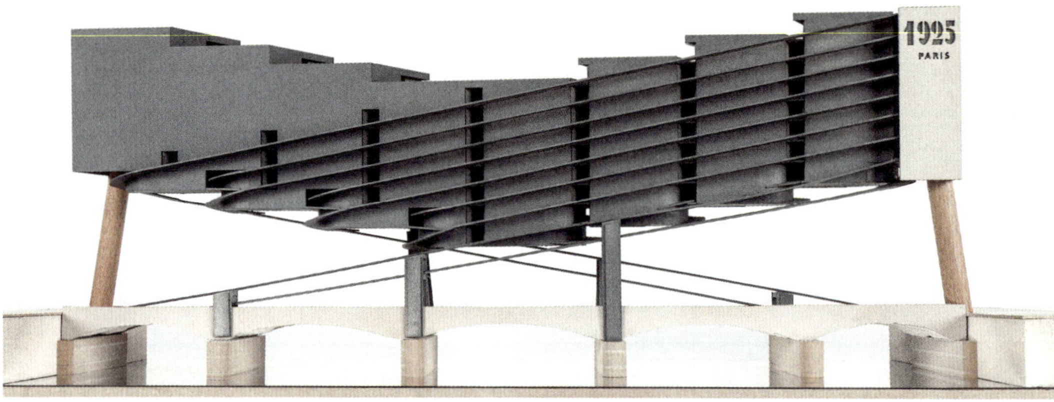

A close relative of El Lissitzky's Wolkenbügel in Moscow, this 1,000-car parking garage is set over one of the Seine's historic bridges. Superimposed onto the existing city, it explores a new language for a high-energy industrial society and reflects not only transportation needs but also the graphic identity of emerging car companies like Citroën and Peugeot. The twelve levels of the garage are connected by outer ramps that define the building's image of architecture in motion, with cars continuously moving up and down. The building cantilevers from a central part, with two atlantes anchoring the ends and providing additional support. The ramps curving across the building are independent of the horizontal surfaces: Accesses appear along the facade, and a single ramp leading up from the city level branches out, allowing access to all the floors. In plan, the ramps form intersecting circles – a recurring motif in Melnikov's work.

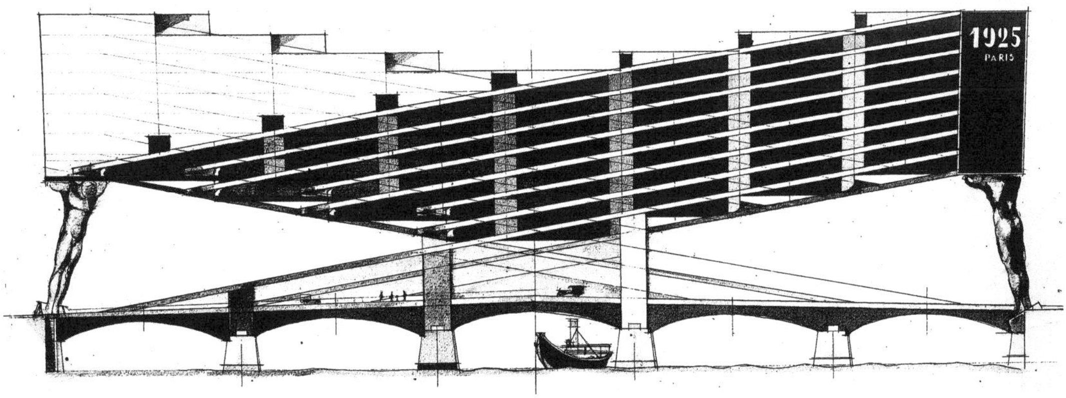

Elevation

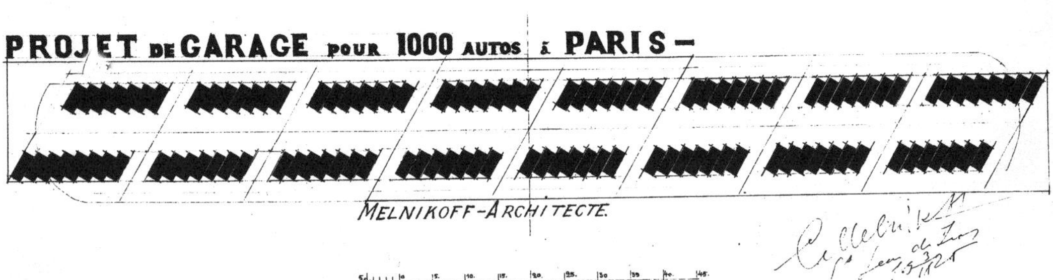

Floor plan of levels 5 to 9 with parking spaces

Garage Cube for 1,000 Cars
Unbuilt
Paris, 1925

Garage Cube for 1,000 Cars
Unbuilt
Paris, 1925

Robin Carnal,
Monica Heleno Oliveira (top)
Scale 1:100

Nicolas Keldany
Keon Ho Lee (bottom)
Scale 1:100

This cubic design for a 1,000-car parking garage incorporates four spiral ramps – geometrically identical but interwoven to create a striking illusion of complexity. Their crossover creates a revolutionary dynamic in a space that is typically boring: the parking garage. Each "snaking" ramp begins on one side of the square and moves in a single direction – two up, two down – hidden behind opaque walls. A small facade opening offers a fleeting glimpse of a car's curved path, hinting at motion without fully revealing it. The tension between the rigid facade and the flowing ramps turns the garage into a theater of movement. The project reflects Melnikov's interest in literal and symbolic motion.[1]

1 See Garrido, *Mélnikov en París*; and Baldeweg and Jaque, *Konstantin Melnikov: aparcamiento para 1000 autos. 2a variante. París, 1925.*

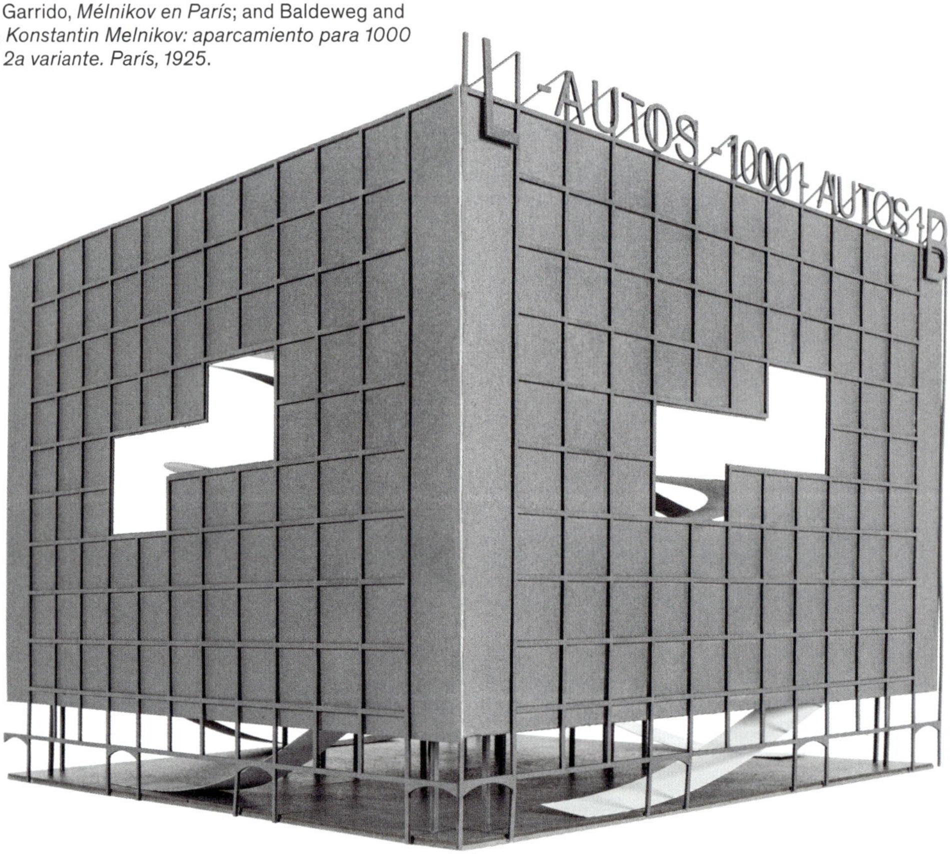

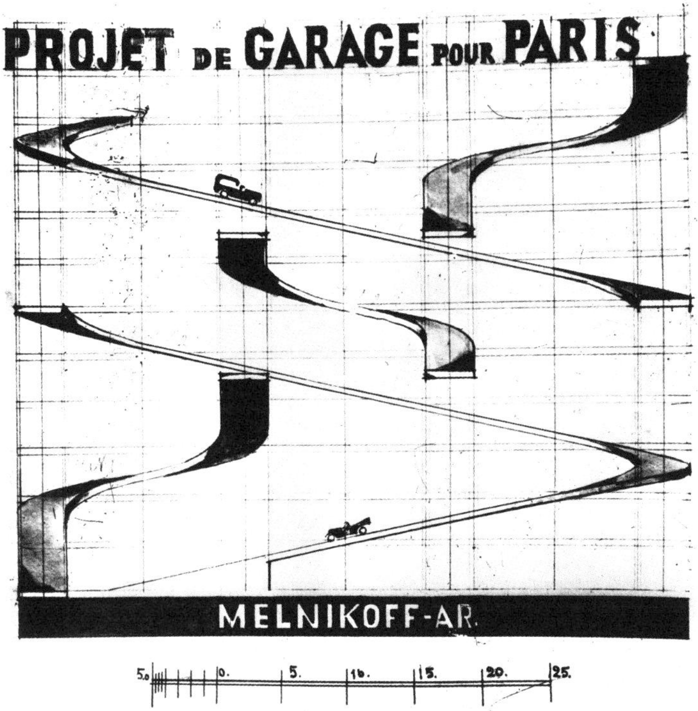

Section showing the ramps

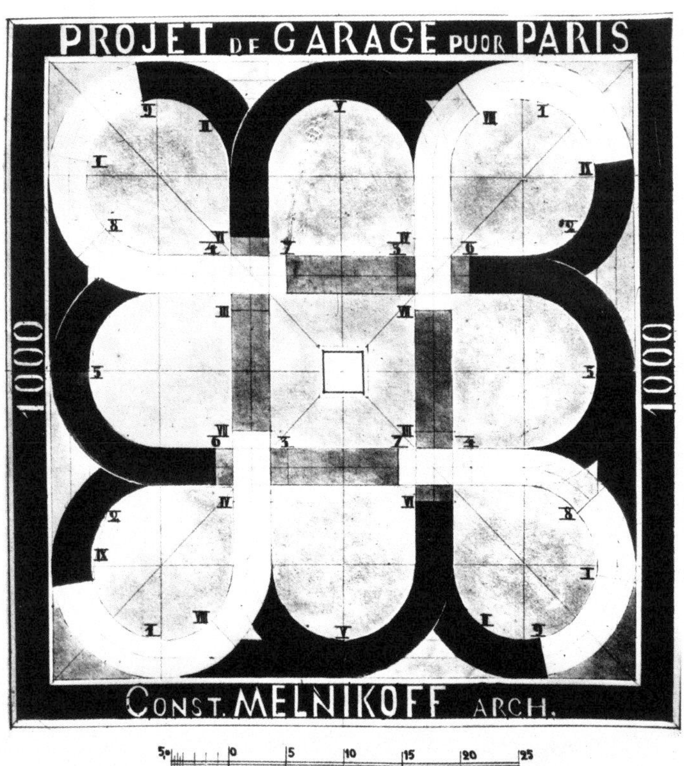

Plan showing the ramps

Bakhmetevsky Bus Garage
Moscow, 1926–1928

Mathias Narbel
Scale 1:100

Bakhmetevsky Bus Garage
Moscow, 1926–1928

Angelo De Angelis
Eleonora Maria Cerri
Scale 1:150

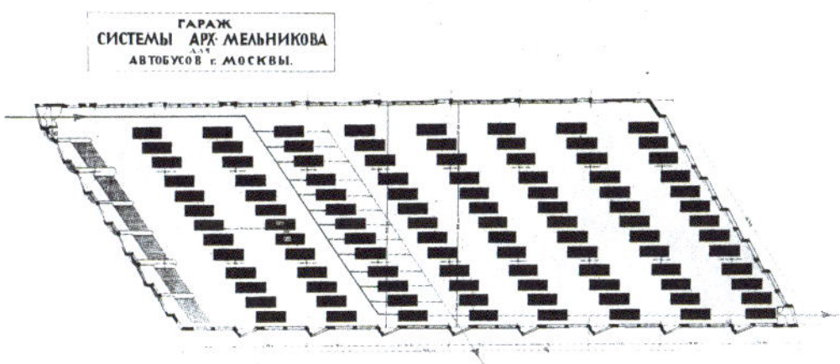

Plan showing bus circulation and parking lots

To accommodate British Leyland buses bought by the Moscow City Council, Melnikov replaced the typical rectangular garage with a rhomboid plan. A "straight-through movement" system reduced turning angles from 90 degrees to 53 degrees, minimizing the need for maneuvering and reversing. Buses entered on one side and exited on the other, parking diagonally along stepped lanes. Despite initial resistance to this concept, test runs on a marked lot proved its efficiency. Renowned engineer Vladimir Shukhov advised on the metal trusses, which spanned 52 meters. Intersecting skylights turned the garage into a luminous temple of transport.

Novoryazansky Truck Garage
Moscow, 1926–1928

Anna Suominen
Scale 1:200

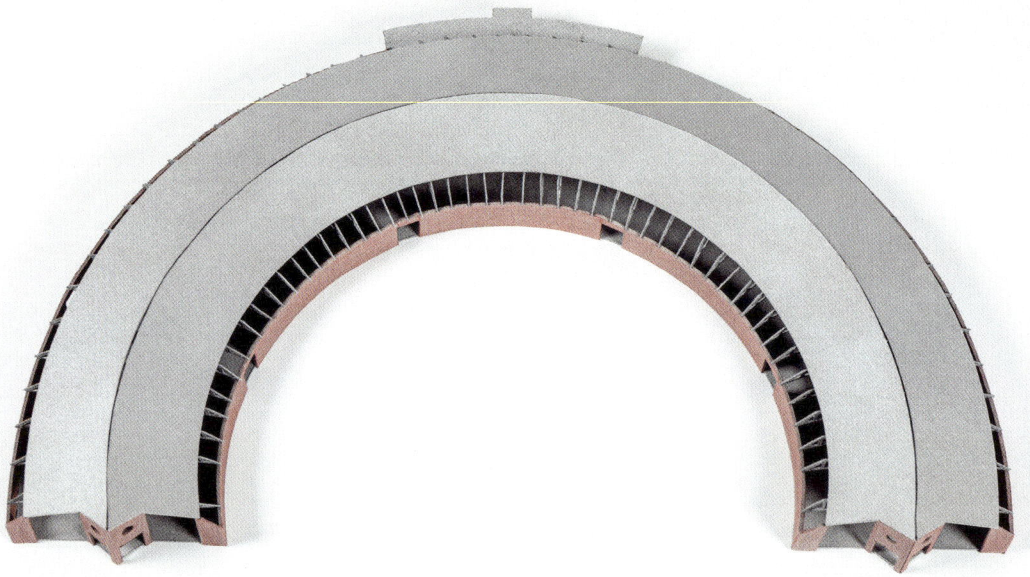

Due to the constraints of a triangular plot, Melnikov designed this truck garage in a horseshoe shape. Early versions followed the "straight-through movement" system of his Bakhmetevsky bus garage, but the final plan adopted a circular movement system inspired by the turntables at locomotive depots. Trucks moved along the "horseshoe" building to and from the main street, and through side doors across the courtyard to the repair workshops. The 150-meter-long semicircular brick structure, with keel-shaped ends touching the street, uses steel trusses to create a column-free interior for unobstructed circulation. A continuous skylight between the wall and roof highlights movement.

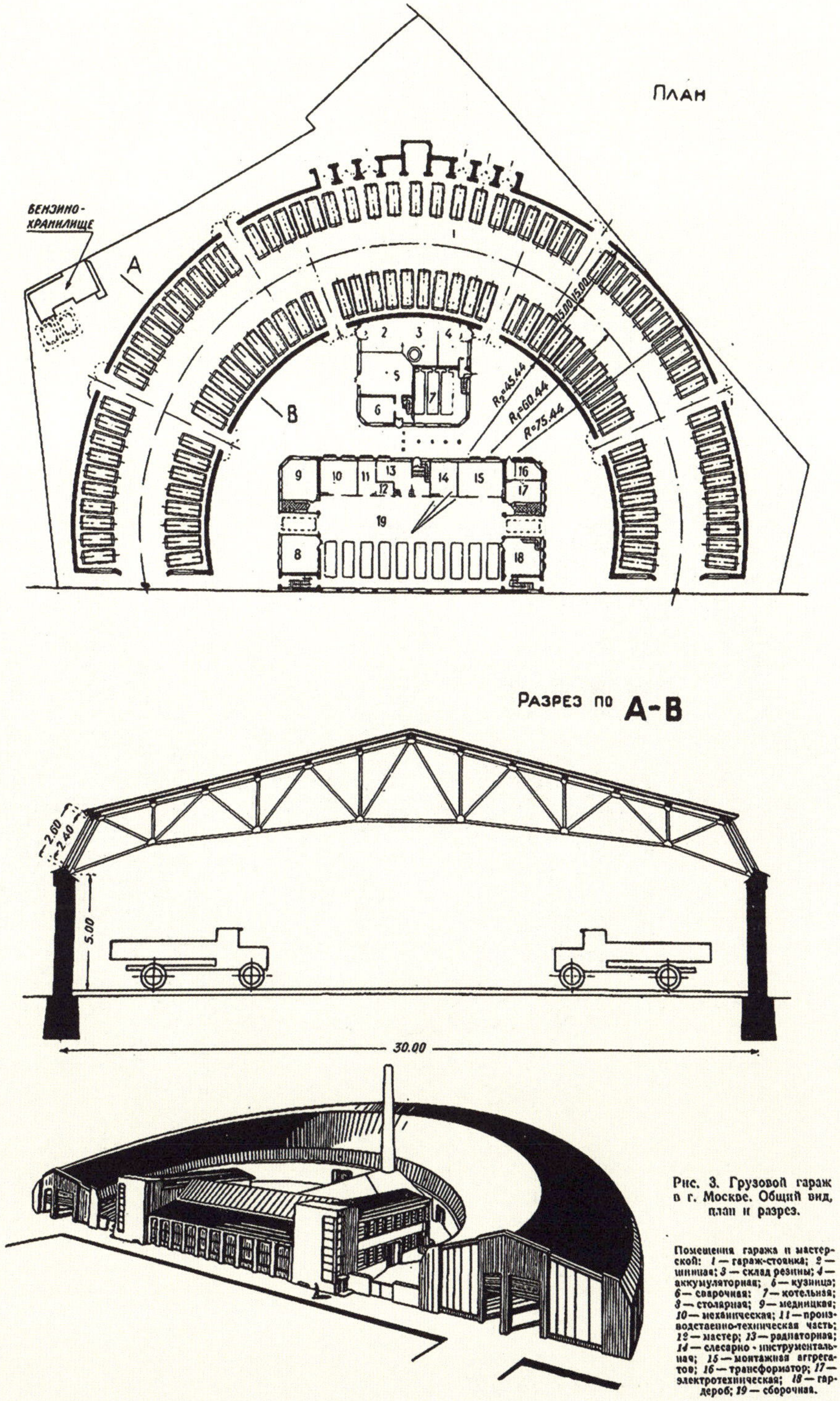

Plan, cross section and general view of the truck garage showing parking spaces

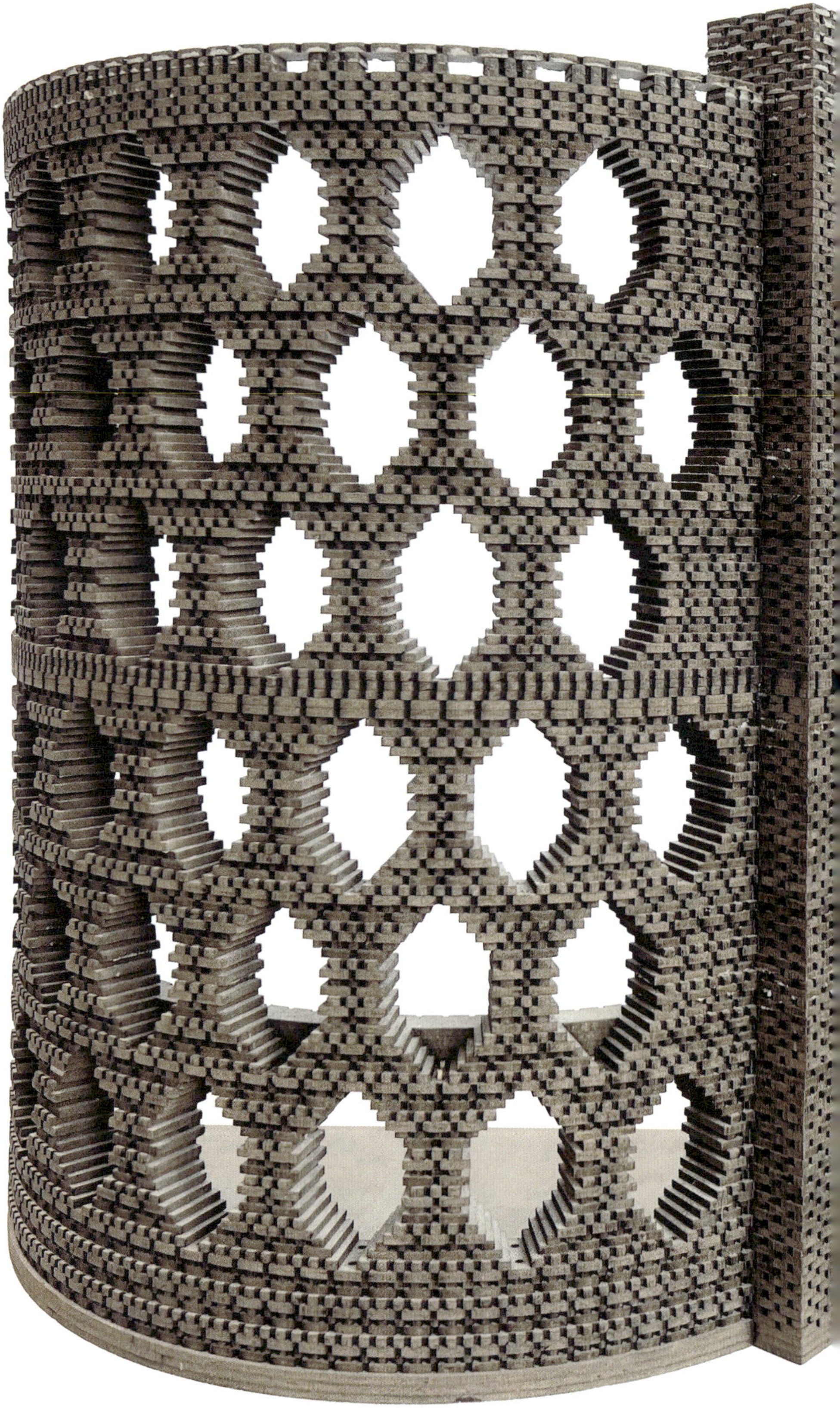

Melnikov House
Moscow, 1927–1929

I-hsuan Chu
Zhiyuan Jiang
Yuxuan Zhang
Scale 1:40

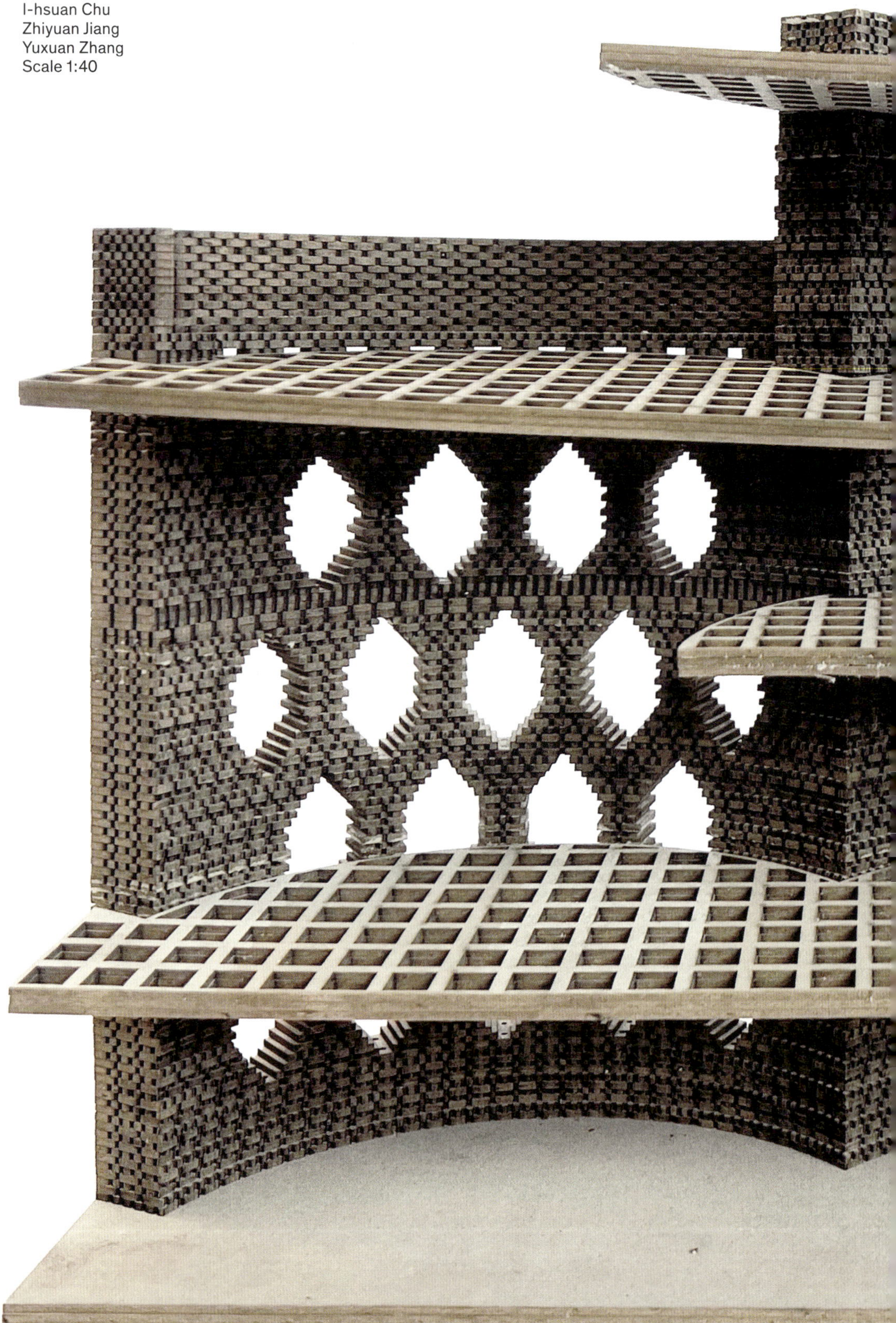

Melnikov House
Moscow, 1927–1929

The Melnikov house-studio, probably one of the most unusual living spaces in the world, represents a brave experiment conducted by the architect on himself and his family.

The outer circular walls, whose unique brick structure is perforated by 120 hexagonal apertures to save on materials and budget, are defined by the interaction of simple cylindrical forms. In turn, in the course of construction the structure defined the facades and the design of fenestration with four types of hexagonal windows.

Light wooden cassettes were employed for the intermediate floors and roof structures. These were prefabricated and assembled on-site. Just touching the external walls along the perimeter, they literally "hang" in the air, spanning almost 10 meters of wide space without any beams or columns. Covered on both sides by tongue-and-groove ceiling and flooring boards, these inexpensive but reliable structures are an illustration of Melnikov's architecture beyond the possible.

Horizontal and vertical structures work together, helping to realize Melnikov's aphoristic expression: "The essence of my house is in equivalence and equability of [structural] tensions, light, air and heat."[1]

1 Konstantin Melnikov, manuscript, Melnikov House archive, inv. 1046 (1961).

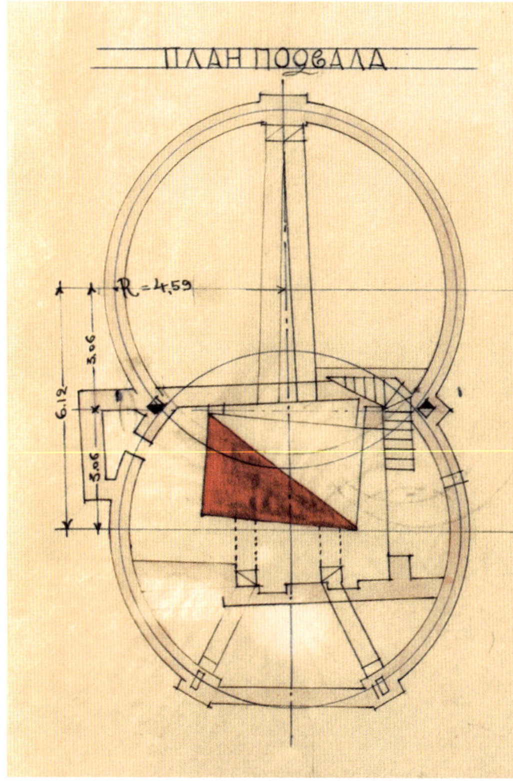

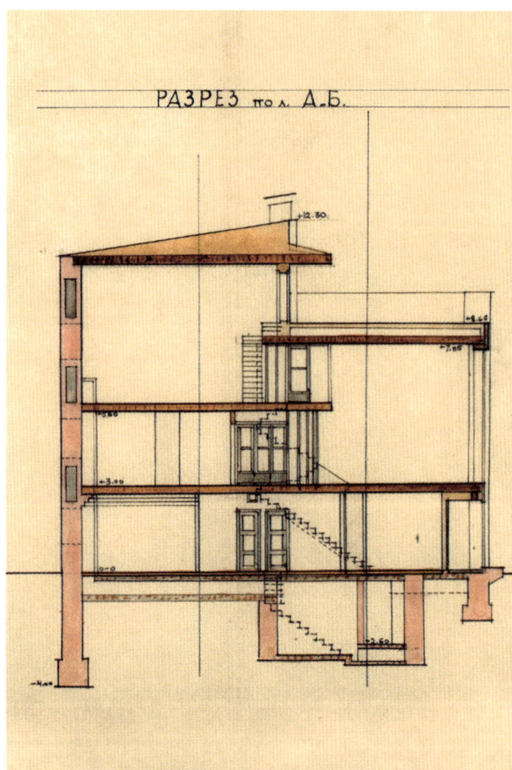

Basement plan (top) and longitudinal section (bottom)

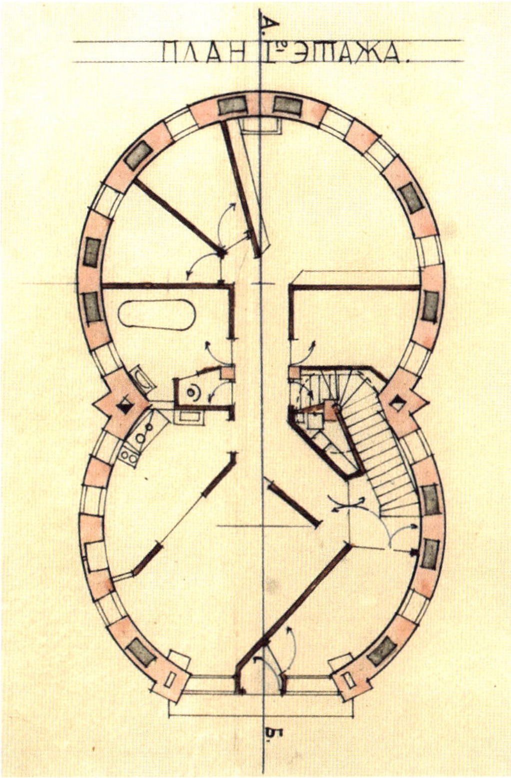

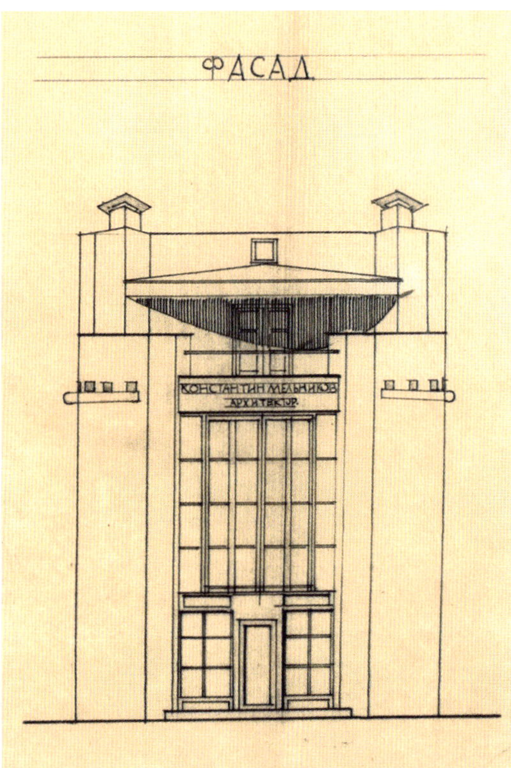

First floor plan (top) and street elevation (bottom)

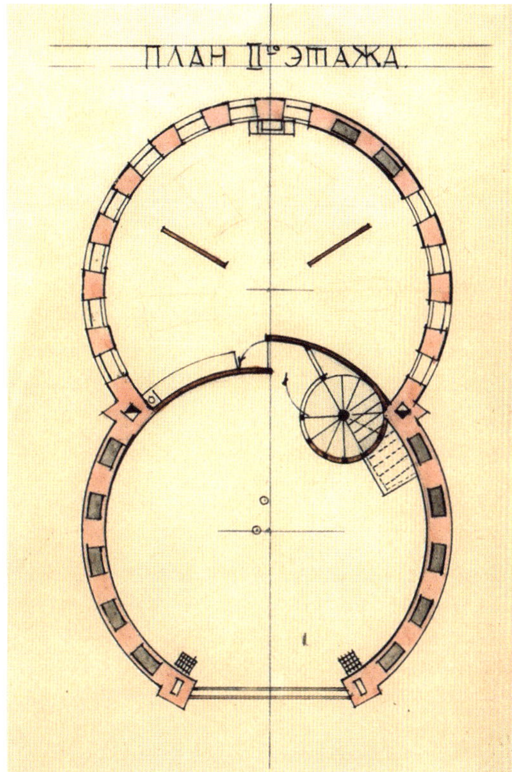

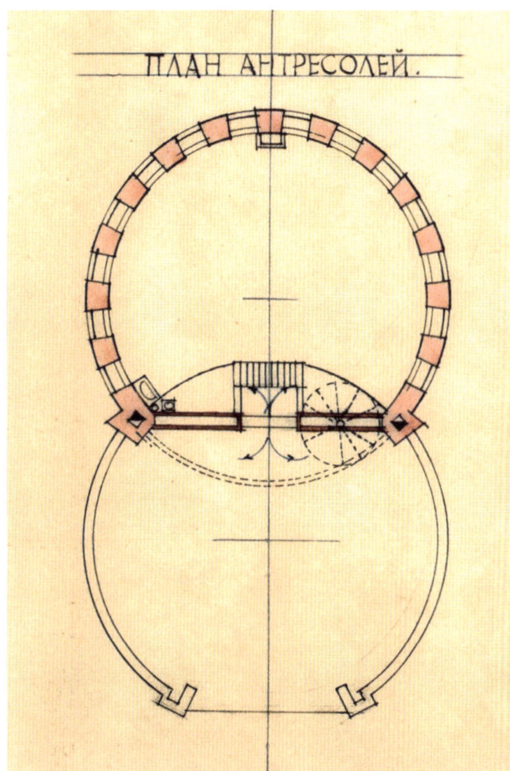

Second floor plan (top) and entresol and terrace plan (bottom)

The three-level house has a hierarchical vertical composition, with spaces for everyday family life on the first level, living space and a sleeping laboratory on the next floor, and the sanctuary-like architect's studio on top.

The main cylindrical rooms of the house are a living room with 5-meter-high walls and one large 4-by-5-meter window; a common bedroom partitioned by wall screens – a laboratory of sleep, which was designed for the whole family; and a temple-like studio, similar in size to the living room, but lit completely differently, with well-diffused natural light coming in through 38 hexagons.

Melnikov gave his house a rigid outer shell but complete interior freedom. The brick cylinder walls carry all the load, allowing a free, flexible plan inside. None of the inner walls are structural, and the 120 hexagonal openings can be opened or closed at will, adapting light, air and space. The result is a truly transformable home ready to evolve with its residents' needs over time.

Michele Christoph Blaser
Lucia Thea Zanti
Scale 1:1

Ekaterina Kolesova
Dea Trapaidze
Scale 1:5

Sofia Karamysheva
Elisaveta Trudova
Scale 1:5

Brick construction

Zuev Workers' Club
Competition entry
Moscow, 1927

Zuev Workers' Club
Competition entry
Moscow, 1927

Edi Chen Yuen-shan Scheidegger
Scale 1:100

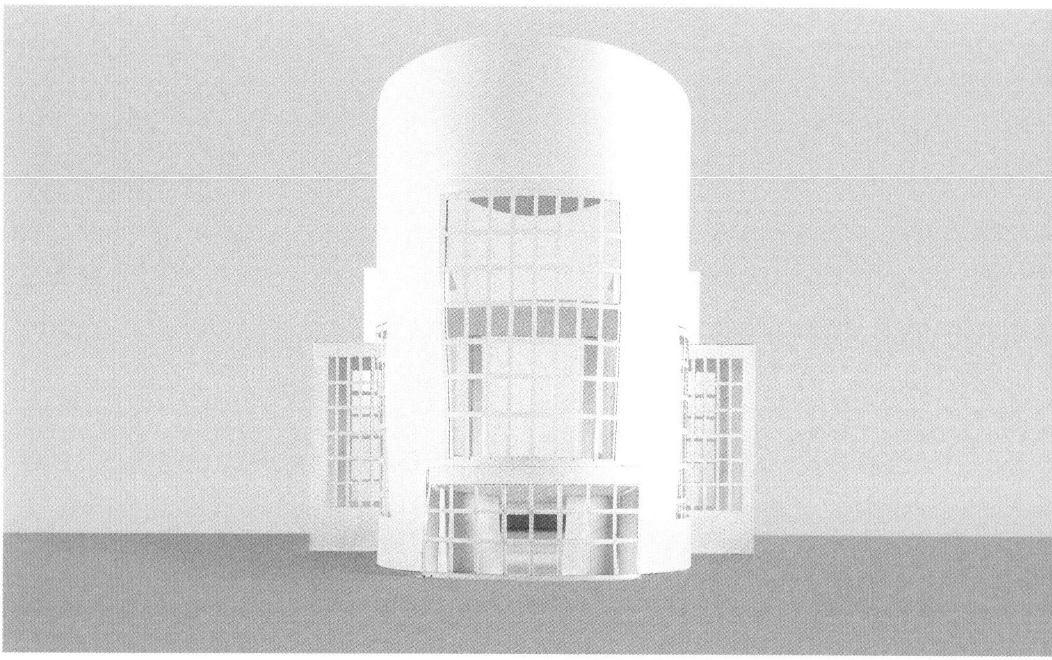

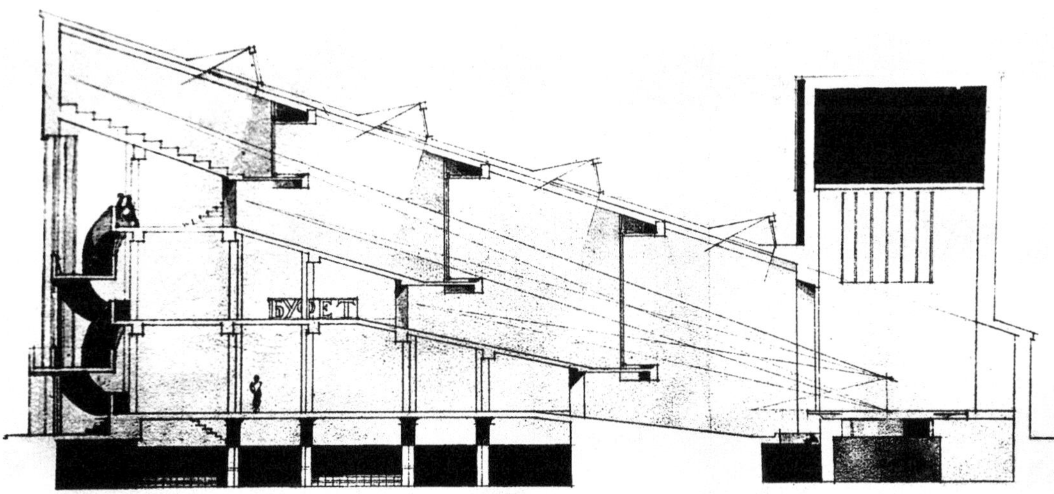

Longitudinal section

Second floor plan

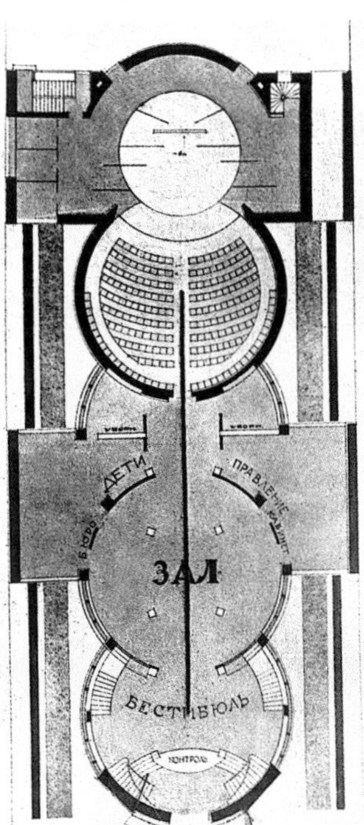

The only unbuilt club of Melnikov's seven. He lost this competition to his friend Ilya Golosov, who also employed a cylindrical form but only to mark the key corner. Commissioned by the same trade union as the famous Rusakov Club, Melnikov's design is a chain of five interlocking cylinders of descending height, cut diagonally – "a musical organ," he said.[1] Two rectangular blocks pierce the cylinders, balancing mass and light. The lowest cylinder houses the stage, gaining height through its connection to a block. Movable walls can transform five intimate round halls into one long auditorium. Though unrealized, this bold interplay of cylinders reappears in later works, especially his iconic house-studio. The curved street facade reveals a spiral staircase behind vertical glazing, flanked by spaces for the club's posters.

1 Konstantin Melnikov, "Architecture of My Life," manuscript, Melnikov House archive, inv. 1060 (1967).

Rusakov Workers' Club
Moscow, 1927–1929

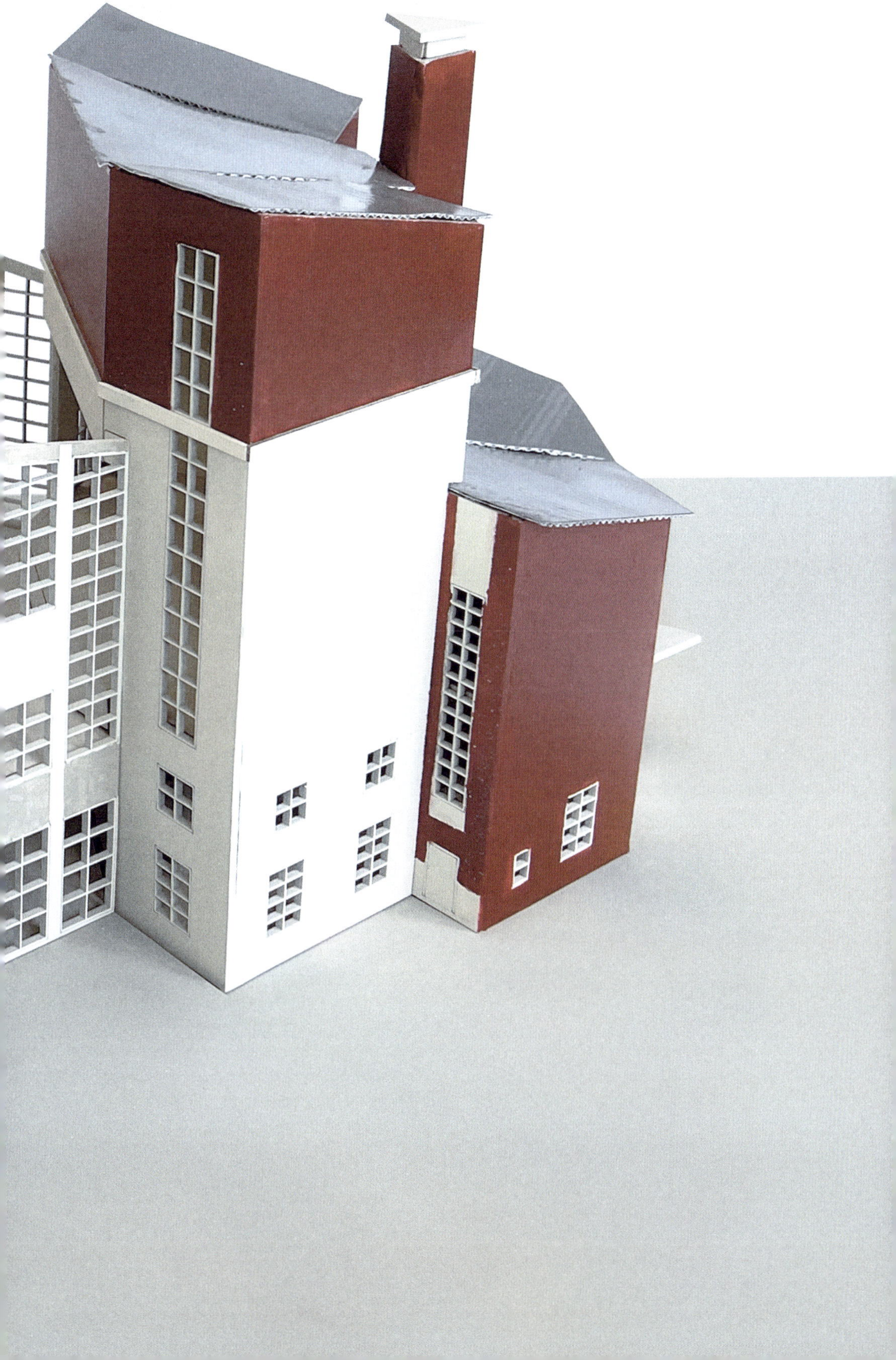

Rusakov Workers' Club
Moscow, 1927–1929

Candice Jacquet
Julian Nehmert (top)
Scale 1:100

Elisa Acquistapace
Nadine Bein (bottom)
Scale 1:100

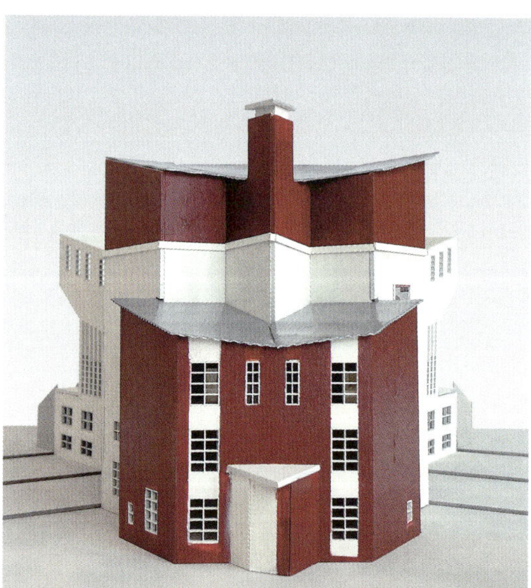

The concept of immediate interior transformation culminated in the sliding floors and walls of Melnikov's seven workers' clubs (1927–1931). Spaces were zoned vertically with raisable floors in auditoriums and horizontally with retractable "living walls," as in the Rusakov Club, where the main hall could be transformed into a combination of rooms for from 350 to 1,225 people. Some projects incorporated retractable floors with pools below, allowing an auditorium to become a water stadium with stands. Outpacing engineering and financial limits, most of these mechanisms remained on paper; the living walls functioned only briefly in Rusakov. A triangular layout with three cantilevered balconies gives the facade a striking megaphone- or cogwheel-like look – an iconic case of *architecture parlante.*

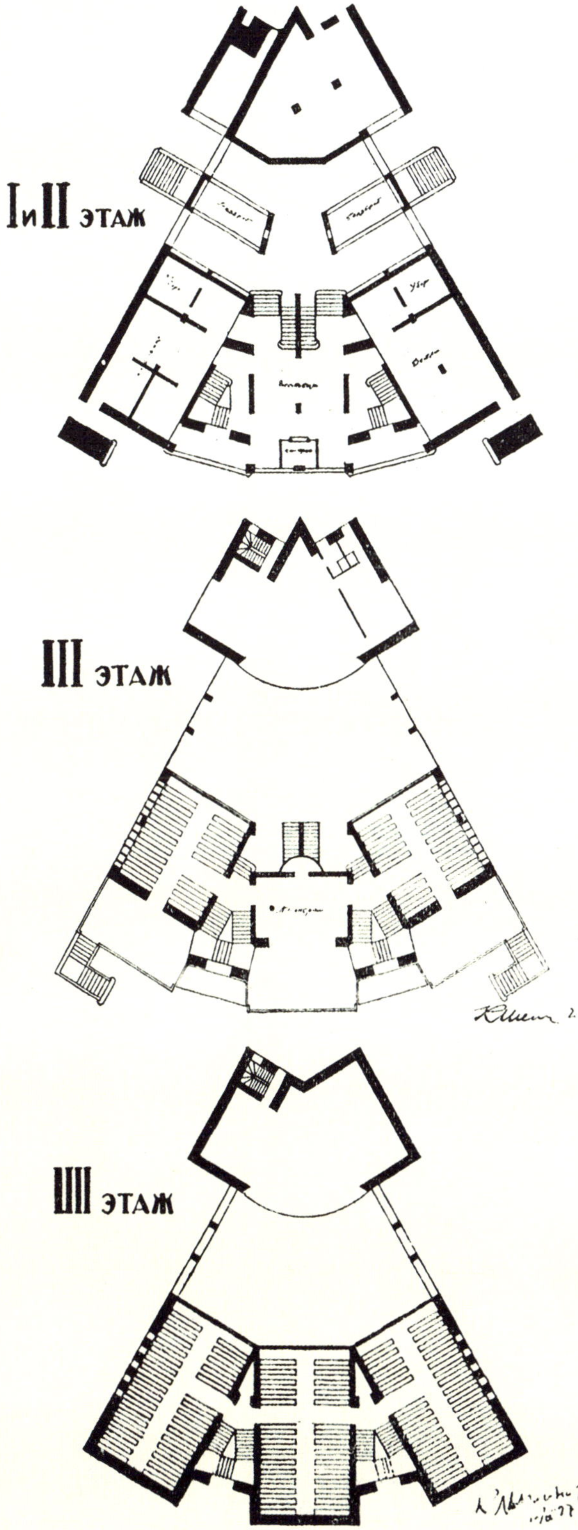

Floor plans of first to third floor, from top to bottom

Kauchuk Workers' Club
Moscow, 1927–1929

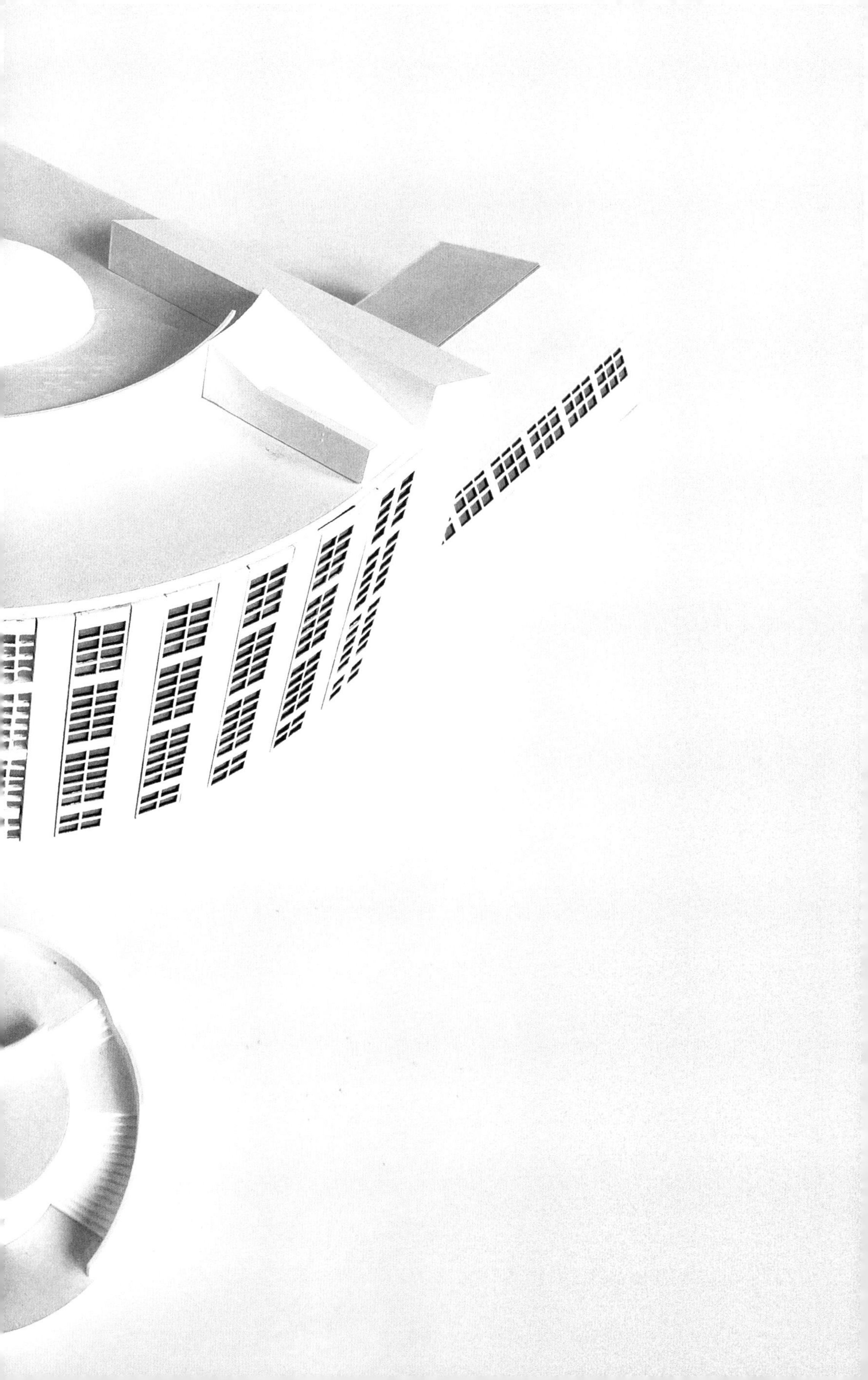

Kauchuk Workers' Club
Moscow, 1927–1929

Mario Poma
Elena Robatto
Scale 1:100

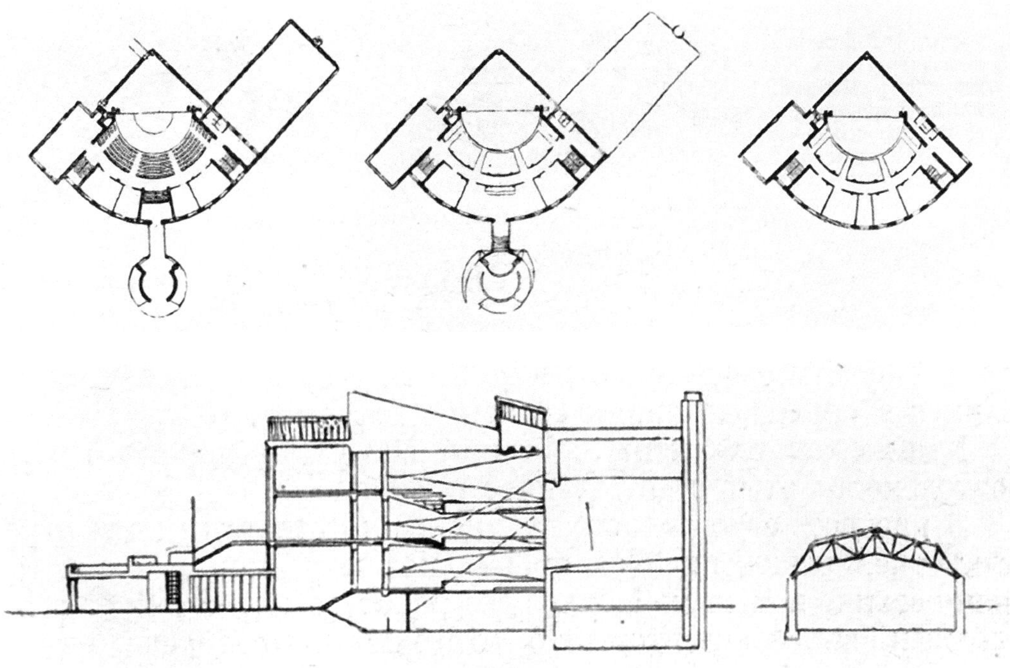

Floor plans (top) and sections (bottom)

This club is based on a quarter-circle plan, curving outward toward the street crossing – inviting rather than dominating. A small, freestanding circular entrance pavilion, pushed forward and flanked by twin open staircases, separates the flows of people with the help of a covered walkway leading to the building behind it. This space also serves as a public tribune for demonstrations. Rhythmic vertical fenestration emphasizes the curve, concealing an amphitheater-like auditorium reminiscent of Shakespeare's Globe. Its cantilevered balconies, equidistant from the stage, were originally intended to function as separate rooms with the help of movable curtains. An unfolding section of floor allowed the semibasement to be used together with or apart from the main space – for dancing or lectures. Although never realized, the stage was meant to rise to balcony level, freeing the lower tiers for mass gatherings. A rooftop terrace extended the club's public space. The club balances rather than opposes the church it faces across the intersection.

Burevestnik Workers' Club
Moscow, 1927–1930

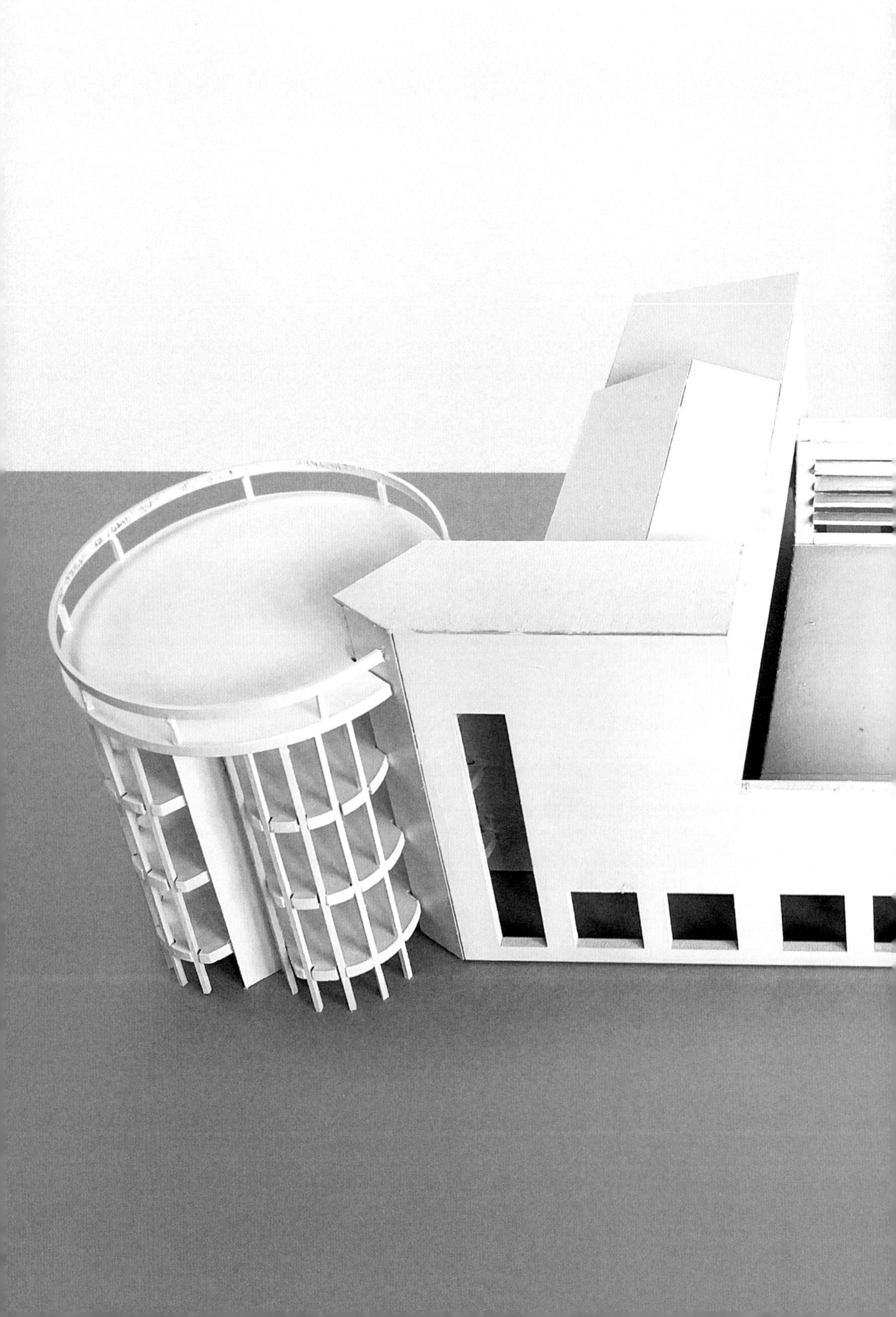

Burevestnik Workers' Club
Moscow, 1927–1930

Rune Meesenburg
Scale 1:100

This club for shoe factory workers is marked by a nearly freestanding five-petal tower crowned with an elegant solarium terrace – a symbol of sunbathing as a part of a healthy lifestyle and a preventive for tuberculosis. The tower's interiors, intended for small group activities, could be rearranged by moving wall screens around a central pillar. A rectangular main volume connects to the tower but follows its own spatial logic. The gymnasium and auditorium were designed to either function independently or be combined into a single space. By folding away the intermediate floor, the auditorium and the swimming pool below it could operate as a water stadium. This multifunctional intent is readable in the longitudinal tiered seating rows along both sides of the auditorium.

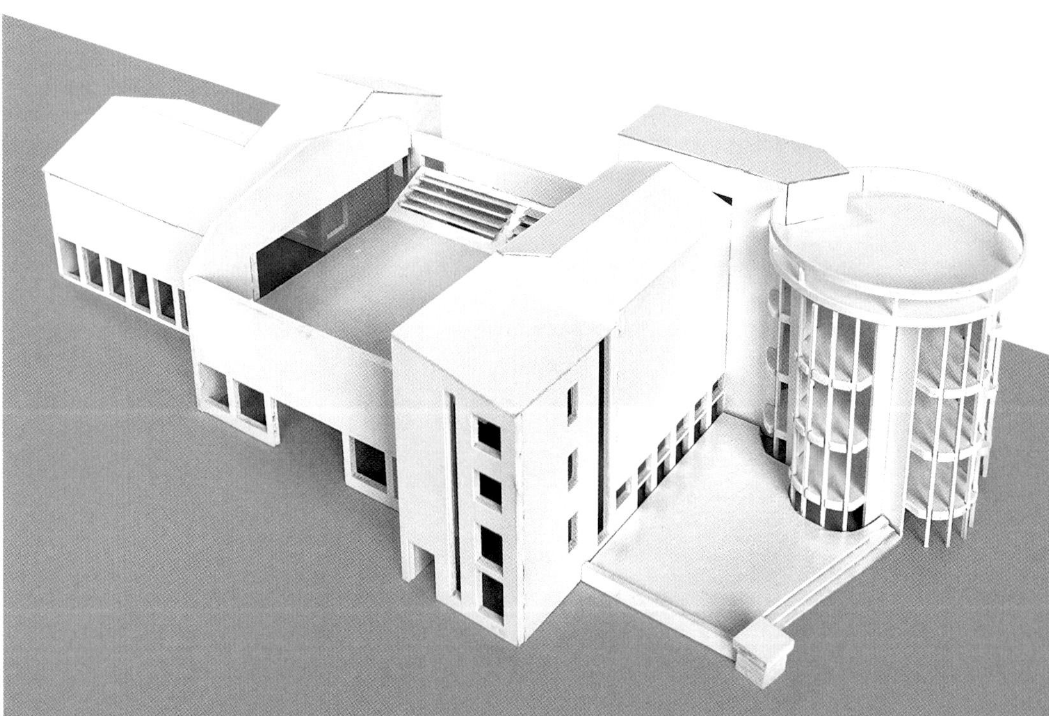

CLUB « BOURENCOSTNIK »
A MOSCOU
ARCHITECTE: K. MELNIKOW

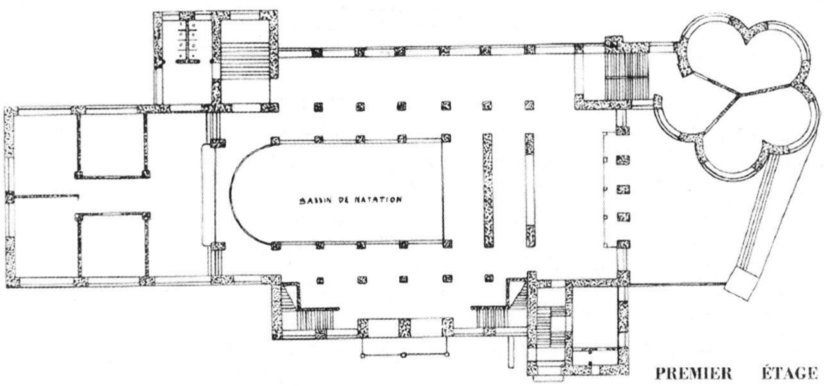

PREMIER ÉTAGE

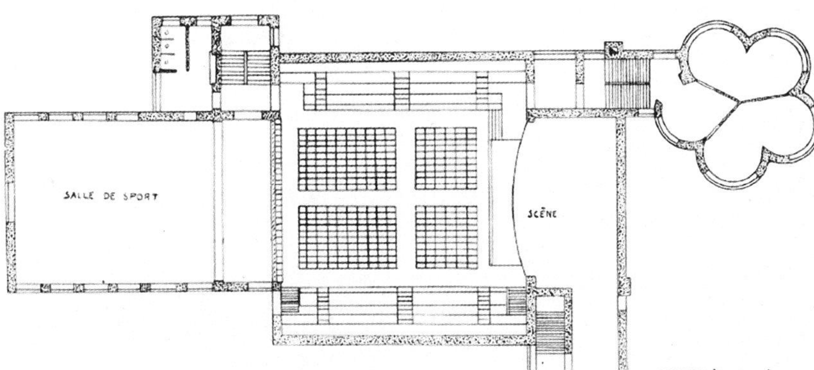

18

DEUXIÈME ÉTAGE

Photo of the general view, taken at the end of the 1920s (top) with the first and second floor plans (bottom)

Svoboda Workers' Club
Unbuilt version
Moscow, 1927

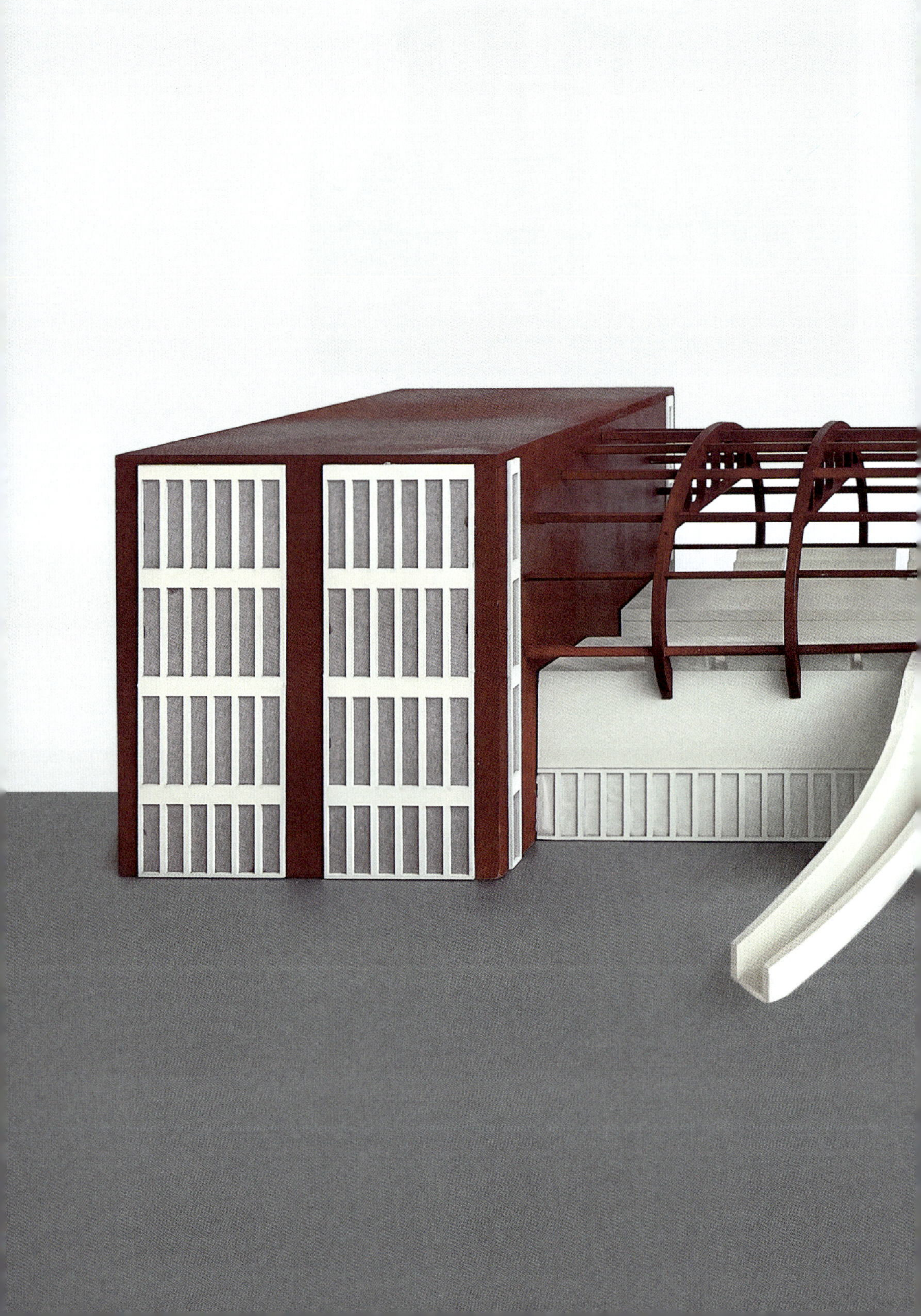

Svoboda Workers' Club
Unbuilt version
Moscow, 1927

Stefania Archilli
Maria Vittoria Giani
Scale 1:100

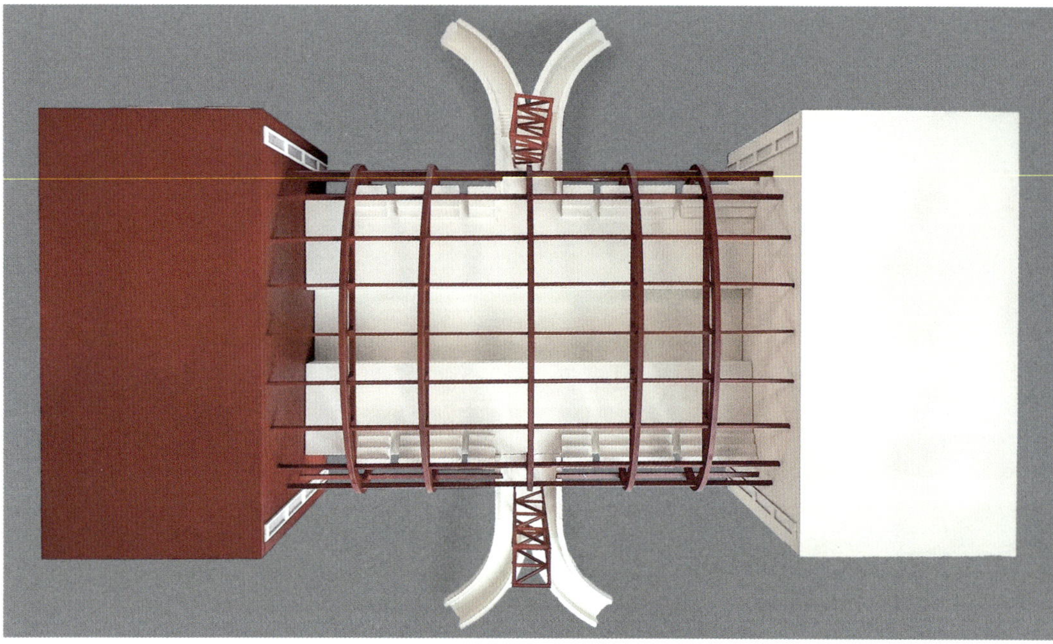

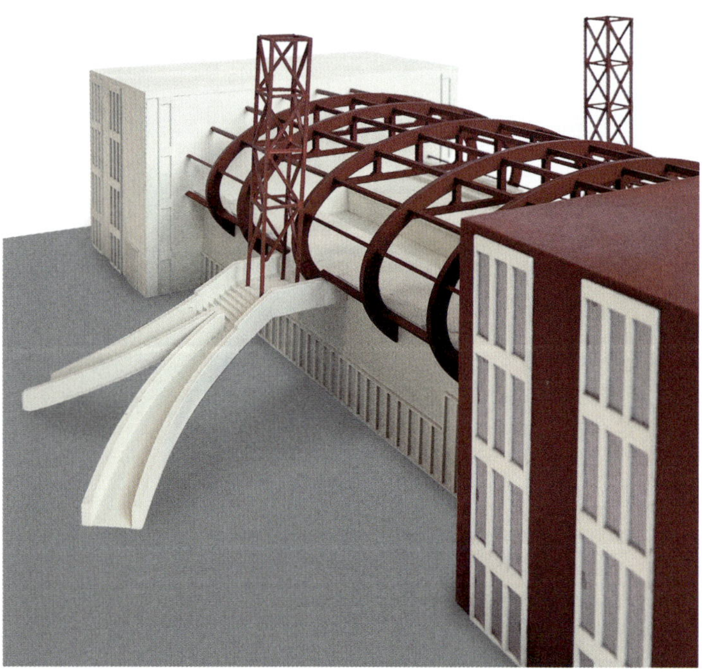

Originally conceived as a cigar-shaped volume flanked by rectangular blocks, this club for the workers of a perfume factory alluded to industrial soap and cosmetics tanks. Two pairs of curved ramps were designed for mass processions, leading directly to the auditorium from both the street and the park sides. In the built version, however, the central ellipsoid was reworked into a multifaceted prism with two expressive external staircases – solutions driven, as in Melnikov's other clubs, by emergency exit requirements. Instead of wasting interior space, these staircases became memorable elements of the facades. With the help of a retractable wall, the auditorium for 1,000 spectators could be divided into a theater and a cinema for 500 people each. A 40-meter training pool below was intended to merge with the upper halls, creating a unique water stadium, as in the Burevestnik Club. This multifunctional and convertible space was ahead of its time: The pool was never realized due to the lack of water infrastructure at the time of construction. The project was then realized in changed form from 1927 to 1931.

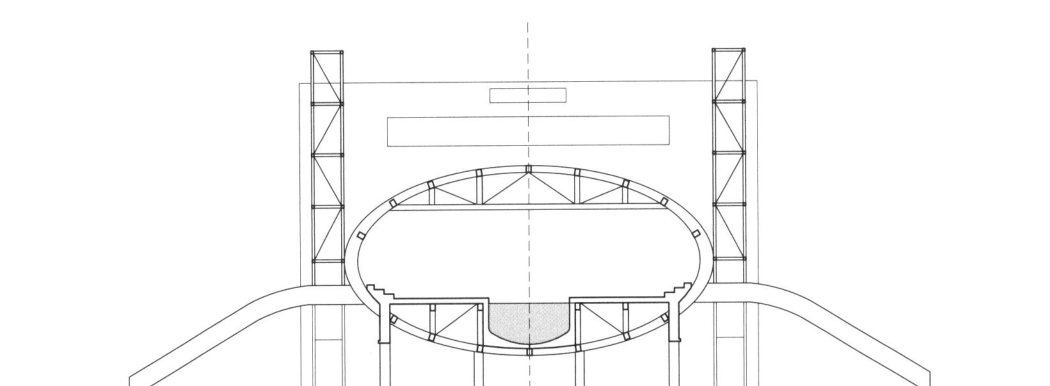

Cross section showing the swimming pool beneath the auditorium floor

Columbus Monument-Lighthouse
Competition entry
Santo Domingo, Dominican Republic, 1929

Gioele Carrera
Stefano Landoni
Scale 1:200

One of 455 competition entries for the Columbus monument-lighthouse, Melnikov's kinetic design fused engineering precision with the spontaneity of nature to symbolize humanity's progress. Two cones – metaphors of the Old and New Worlds – lean into each other, embodying the spirit of Columbus. A chapel with the explorer's remains is affixed to the upper cone, while the lower gives way to dynamic wings. The 200-meter-high structure rotates on its base: Its vanes are periodically set in motion by accumulated energy from rainwater and wind, triggering the broadcast of radio and telegraph messages across the globe – calling on humanity to remember Columbus's legacy.

Two worlds (two cones), one supporting the other. In the midst of these two worlds stands the monument to Columbus, who, by uniting them, awakened the vital force of America. In abundant streams, the sap flows from the top of the cone, through the crown of Spain, along the crystal strings of the monument to Columbus, and pours into the Old World.

Created on the foundation of European civilization, the culture of America is increasingly acquiring independence and creative originality. The support of the Old World (the lower cone) is replaced by new, powerful supports in the form of two receding wings. These mechanized wings cut through the wind and assume a favorable position to balance the dome of the Pan-American Union, each time presenting a new impression to the inhabitants of Santo Domingo.

The greatness of Columbus's discovery of an entire new world, the immensity of its significance, cannot be contained within any permanent form. Therefore, the boundlessness of the architectural action of the monument to Christopher Columbus can only be realized by incorporating into the project's composition — The Forces of Nature.

In the present project, the monument, with the remains of Columbus fixed to the upper cone, may rotate provided that two conditions coincide: the wings align along the diameter, and a certain amount of rainwater collects at the top of the cone. Then one wing closes the valve and stops the stream of water flowing around the monument, while the other wing opens the lower valve, and all the water, with the required pressure, rushes to the turbine beneath the floor, and the monument slowly, slowly …

This may happen once in a hundred years.

The wings lift the cone on seven rings (a gamma); pushing off, they play musically day and night, sending their waves across the surface of the earth, stirring humanity to unceasing creation of great works and feats, as Christopher Columbus did.

K. Melnikov

From the explanatory note for the Columbus monument-lighthouse competition entry, Santo Domingo, 1929

Plan of rooftop terrace and ramps

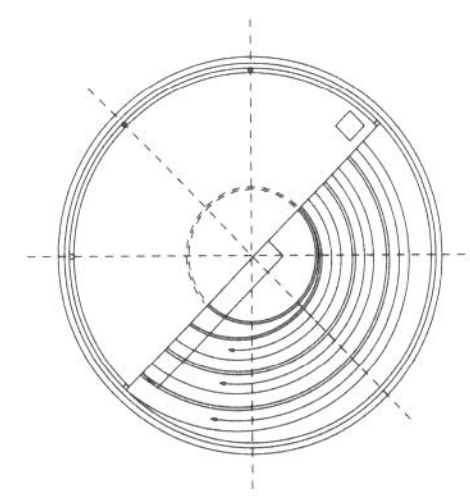

Floor plan: chapel with Columbus's remains

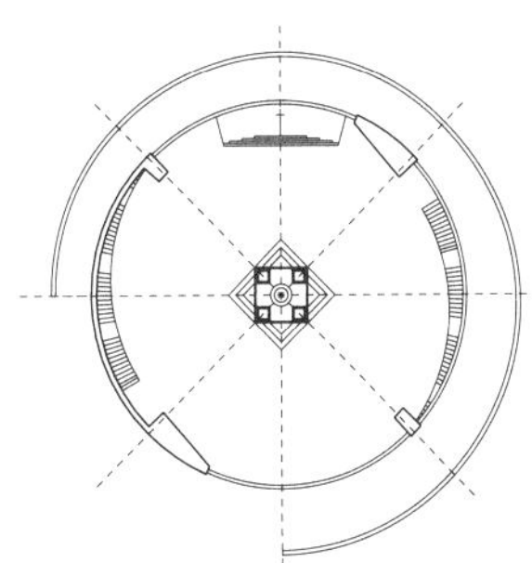

First floor plan, including museum

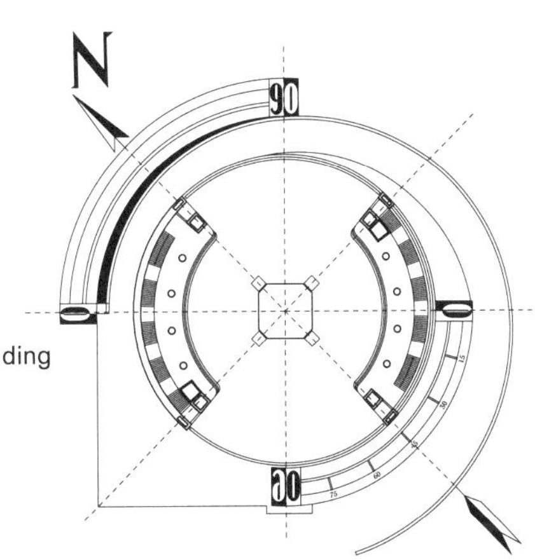

Section

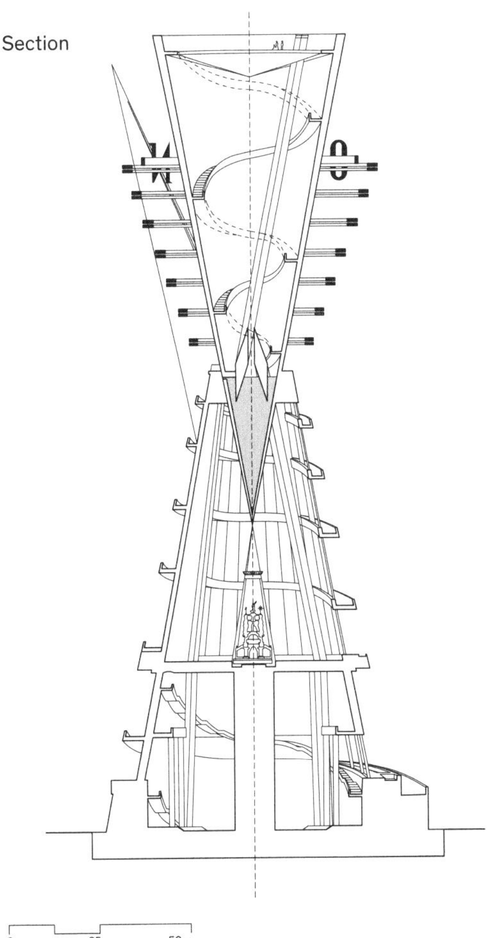

Green City Master Plan
Competition entry
Moscow Region, 1930

ПЛАНИРОВАНИЕ ТЕРРИТОРИИ
ВЫСТАВКИ
АЭРОДРОМ
ВОЕННОЕ
ПОЛЕ
Астафьевская
ОРОД"

Green City Master Plan
Competition entry
Moscow Region, 1930

Sophie-Charlotte Frehse
Agata Kobus
Scale 1:25,000

Wiktor Jerzy Martin
Takehiro Tsumuraya
Scale 1:12,500

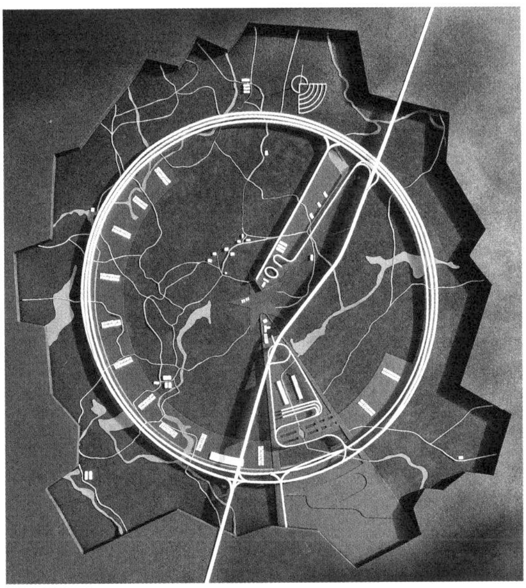

This plan looks less like a technical blueprint than a visionary artwork – a giant circular imprint of humanity on wild nature. Floating icons – a carrot, an oak, a child, an elephant and an ox – form an intuitive infographic collage. A sophisticated ring-and-radial transport scheme organizes the vast resort, edged by "laboratories of sleep," recalling the saltworks semicircle in Claude-Nicolas Ledoux's ideal city. The arrow-shaped sectors evoke El Lissitzky's iconic Russian Civil War poster *Beat the Whites with the Red Wedge* (1919). At the center, a five-pointed star bears the frightening behaviorist label *Institute for Changing the Human Form*. Seeking to posit architecture as a modern path to well-being in direct contact with nature, Melnikov introduced the concept of "rationalized rest." He answered the competition brief not with architecture alone, but with a full "recipe" for renewing human energy by way of medicine, science, poetry and nature.

Green City
Sleeping Sonata Building
Competition entry
Moscow Region, 1930

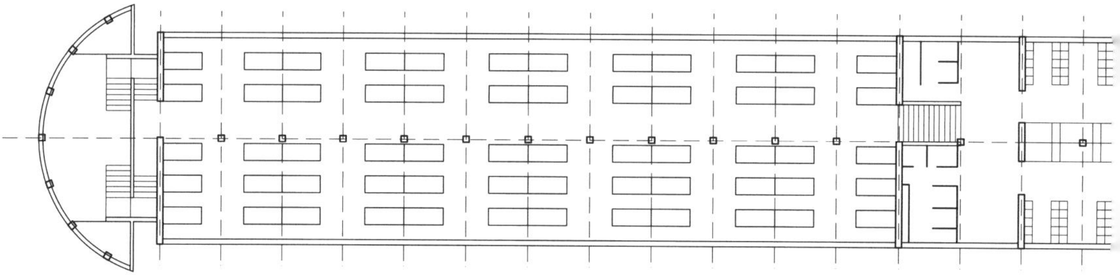

Floor plan

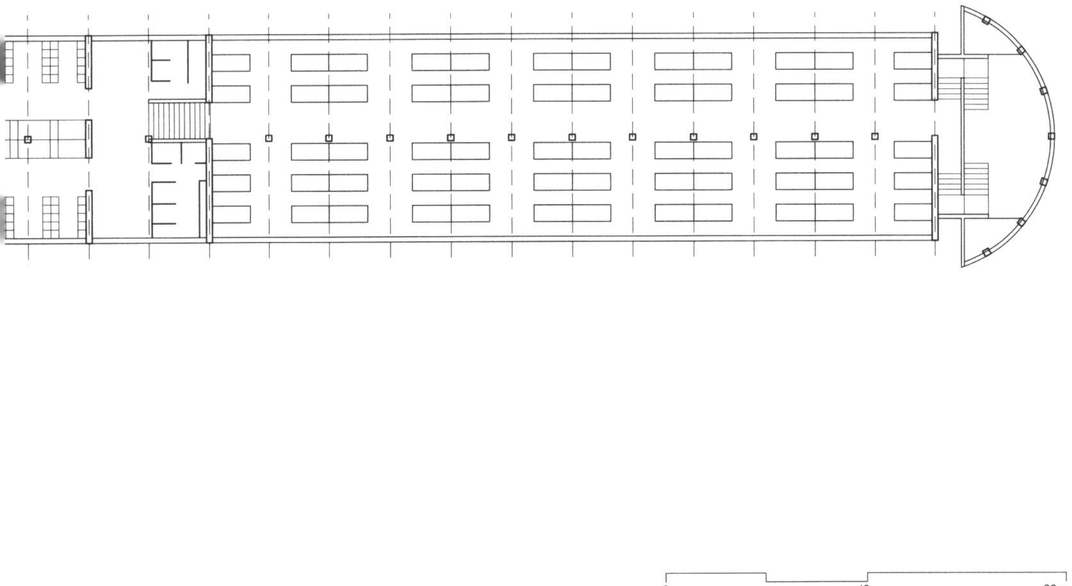
0
10
20 m

Green City
Sleeping Sonata Building
Competition entry
Moscow Region, 1930

Katharina Waechter
Scale 1:100

Melnikov's proposal for the future Green City – a resort near Moscow – responded to Stalin-era industrialization by promoting rest for exhausted workers. At its heart was the Sleeping Sonata, a chamber for collective day sleep. Melnikov saw sleep as life's greatest cure, a daily rebirth. Twelve clusters of interconnected Sonata buildings, each for hundreds of guests, were to be placed along the perimeter of the circular resort. Each "laboratory of sleep" featured inclined beds in gentle motion, along with calming sounds, natural scents and controlled temperature and humidity to induce efficient therapeutic rest. Medics were to monitor the chambers from semicircular control rooms flanking each end of the building. Though never built, the Sonata mixes architecture, medicine, nature and technology into a vision of bodily and spiritual renewal through sleep.

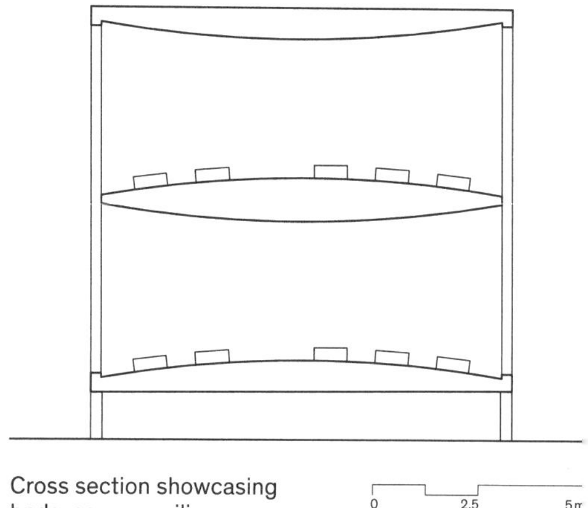

Cross section showcasing beds, convex ceilings and floors

MOSPS Theater
Competition entry
Moscow, 1930–1931

MOSPS Theater
Competition entry
Moscow, 1930–1931

Nastassja Marie Daun
Marlene Fischer
Scale 1:200

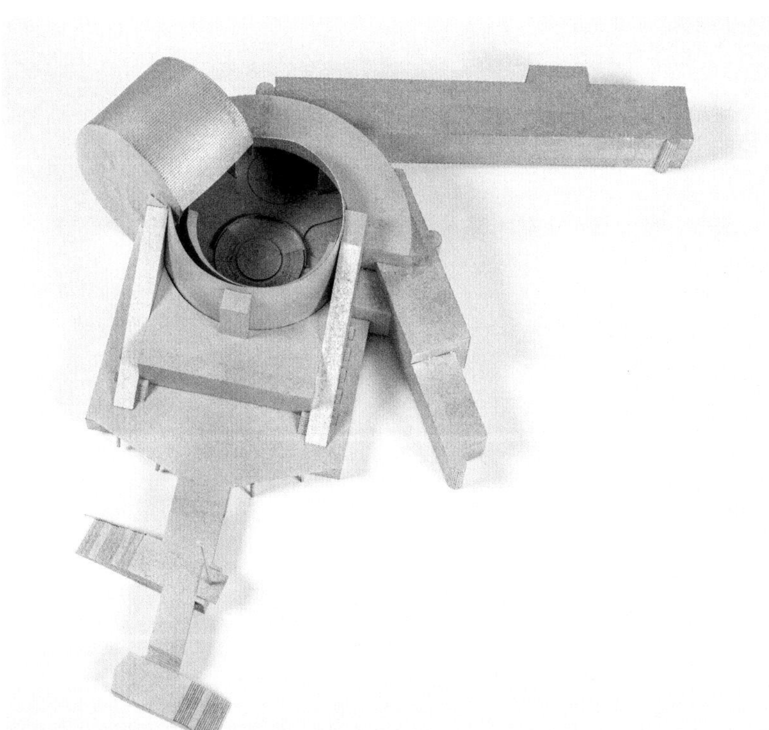

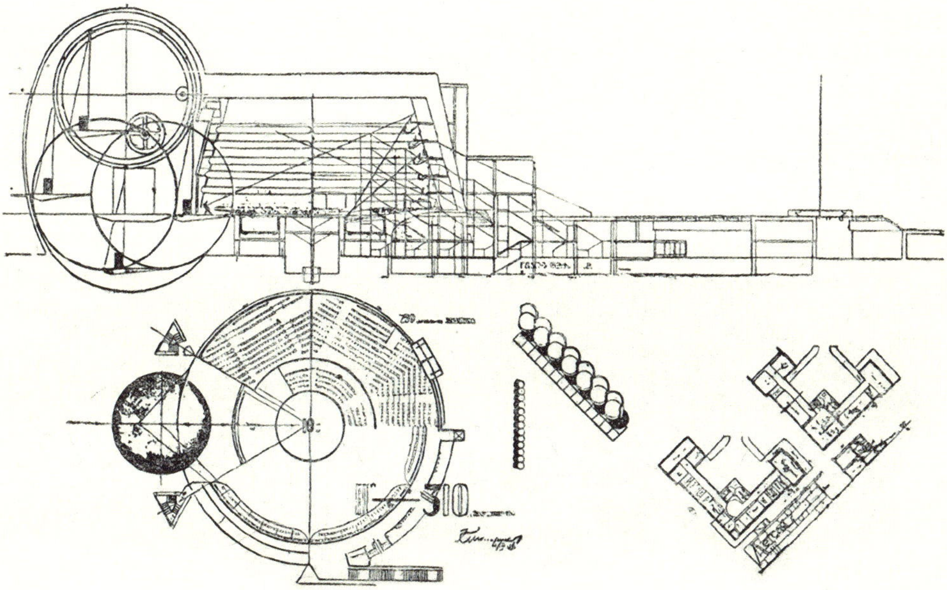

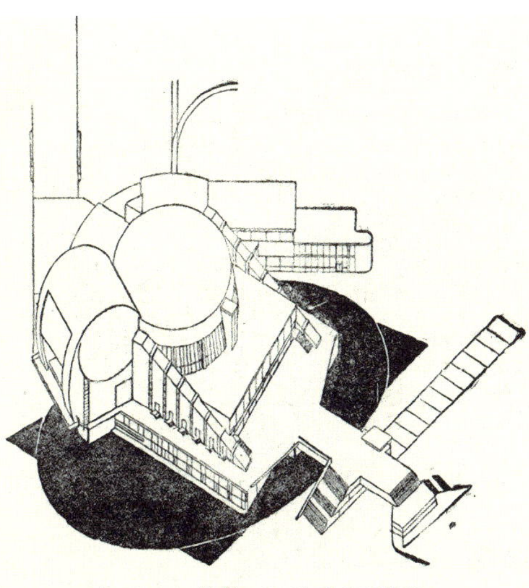

Section and plan (top)
Axonometry (bottom)

At first glance, this looks less like a theater than an orbital station – almost cosmic architecture. A visionary kinetic project powered not by human hands (as in Leningrad Pravda) or natural forces (as in the Columbus monument), but by machines. The seven-tiered auditorium forms a colossal rotating "chair" for 3,000 spectators, turning them toward three separate stages in succession. One of these stages is integrated into a Ferris wheel, allowing vertical scene changes at an astonishing speed, enhanced by water effects and pools. A fourth stage is arranged as an arena. Uniquely, the orchestra and central seating rotate around it, so the conductor always remains aligned with the scene in focus. The project's radical spatial logic recalls Walter Gropius's Total Theater (1927), but here, theatricality is reimagined through motion.

"The aesthetics of the theater are not beauty, but the power of the utmost. What in life is only dreamed of, is realized in the theater … Theater is a dynamic art: The actor moves, his voice moves, light moves – so too must the spectator. To witness incredible speeds of action and remain alive and unscathed – that is the goal of today's performance."[1]

1 Konstantin Melnikov, "Explanatory note to the project of MOSPS Theater," manuscript, Melnikov House archive, inv. 1051 (January 1931), 56–57.

Frunze Military Academy
Competition entry
Moscow, 1931

Marius Gabriel Déprez
Arthur Vincent
Scale 1:50

This project continues the architect's experiments with cylinders as modular forms. The academy is arranged as a zigzagging chain of top-to-bottom glazed volumes – each of which represents a year of study – that are connected horizontally to suggest continuity within the disciplines. The rhythmic repetition of simple forms reflects military aesthetics and order. Melnikov combines both overlapping cylinders, as in his own house-studio, with freestanding units. A star is placed horizontally between the floors of the entrance cylinder, highlighting its symbolic importance. On the opposite end, a cantilevered aula echoes the dramatic massing of then just completed Rusakov Club.

First floor plan

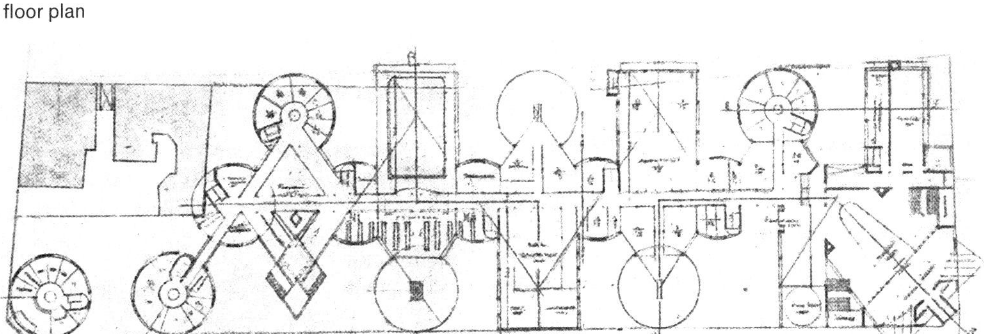

Arbat Square Reconstruction
Unbuilt
Moscow, 1931

Arbat Square Reconstruction
Unbuilt
Moscow, 1931

Mara Mari
Francisco Silva
Scale 1:400

General site plan

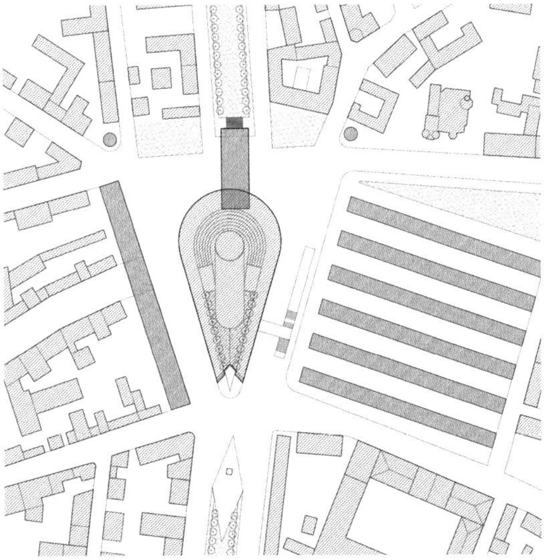

General project plan

This historic square in central Moscow, commissioned to Melnikov to resolve chaotic traffic, was conceived as a multifunctional space: a transport hub, public gathering area and access point for converging streets. Melnikov aimed to prove that the triangle shape – one of his favored forms – could absorb the maximum number of streets. The triangle's apex faced the Gogol monument; its base, Nikitsky Boulevard. The corners were rounded for a smoother flow. The design had two levels: an underground garage with ramps and metro access, and a ground-level amphitheater for mass events, bordered by greenery. Tiered seating reduced noise and maximized sunlight. Six massive parallel structures, decreasing in height, extending from the Kremlin toward the heart of the square, and on the opposite side a building with a monumental arch over Arbat Street, reinforced the triangular layout.

Monumentalism, 1932–1937

After a wave of commissions for clubs and garages in the 1920s, Melnikov soon faced financial and creative difficulties as a freelance architect. Fortunately, in 1932 the Central Asian Communist officials invited the renowned architect to design a Palace of Labor in Tashkent. Nearly two years of work, generous honorariums and a field trip eased his financial troubles. Though never built, this vast, ground-expanded project with multiple volumes of unusual forms marked a transition from his 1920s avant-garde style to a language of new monumentality.

Co-opted by the regime like other leading Soviet architects, Melnikov was appointed head of Architectural Studio No. 7 under the Moscow City Council in 1933. His megaprojects of the time – the Palace of Soviets and the NKTP building – were colossal and wildly out of scale with the city, reflecting the demands of the briefs. His last painful attempt to understand what "socialist realism" meant in architecture, and to please the system, was the design for the USSR pavilion at the 1937 Paris Exposition: monumental in form yet too individualistic in manner to embody the spirit of the collectivist era. Soon after, Melnikov was pushed to the margins and dismissed from teaching, ultimately leaving the stage of Soviet architecture.

Palace of Nations
(a.k.a. Palace of Soviets)
Moscow, 1932

Palace of Nations (a.k.a. Palace of Soviets) Moscow, 1932

Inaya Berger
Hadiseh Karimi
Scale 1:300

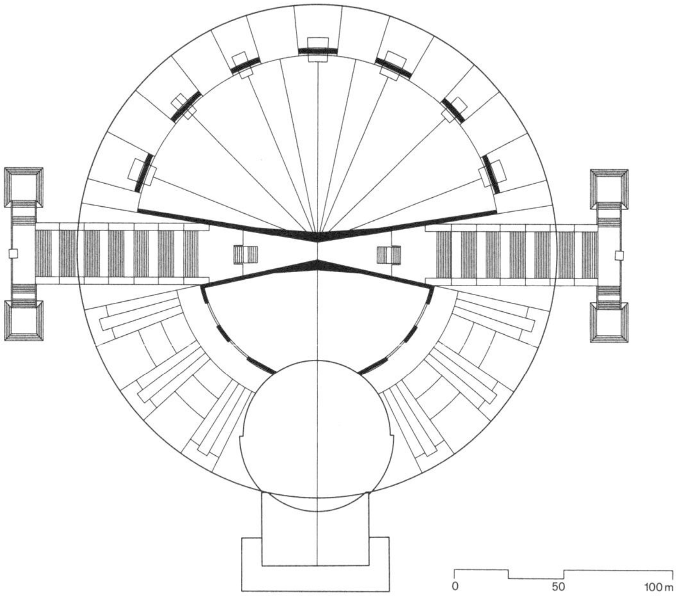

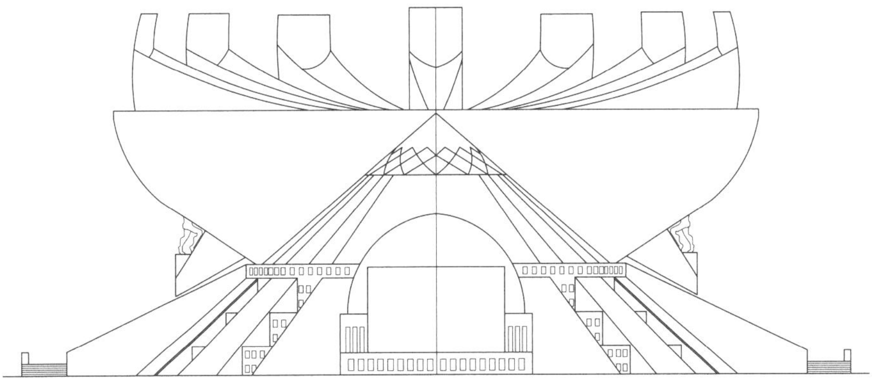

Elevation

0 50 100 m

This reckless project reflects Melnikov's attempt to engage with the emerging Stalinist monumentalism. Several versions were submitted between 1931 and 1933, outside the official competition. He presented it in both graphic and poetic forms: Naïve verses explained the two pyramids – one upright, one inverted – as symbols of the old and new regimes. A schematic social hierarchy, from pharaohs to slaves, was reimagined as two half-cones, one overturned by Revolution. The cup of this cantilevered, unstable cone was symbolically – and structurally – supported by seven pillar-workers bearing the names of the then seven Soviet republics. Melnikov had already employed the cone metaphor in his 1929 Columbus monument-lighthouse design, where the twin forms symbolized the Old and New Worlds.

NKTP Building
(People's Commissariat
for Heavy Industry)
Competition entry
Moscow, 1934

NKTP Building
(People's Commissariat
for Heavy Industry)
Competition entry
Moscow, 1934

Sveva Bonapace
Maura Pagani
Scale 1:500

One of Melnikov's late megaprojects – like the Palace of Nations – was this attempt to align with the cultural revolution's mainstream. The high-rise plan for the powerful Ministry for Heavy Industry was shaped as a double V, symbolizing the Five-Year Plan; later critics saw it as an "M" – his own initial. Just imagining this giant beside the Kremlin takes your breath away – but that was the brief. Open staircases rose through colossal cogwheels at corner entrances, while Atlantean figures crowned fifty-nine floors of offices and public spaces, including a hotel and kindergarten – a city within a city – plus sixteen more underground floors, thanks to a massive excavated pit. Melnikov compared the surprise effect to the *Carmen* overture.

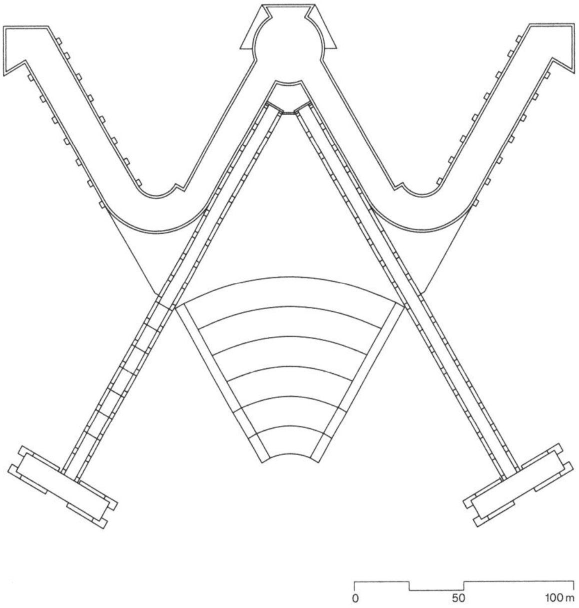

USSR Pavilion for the International
Exposition in Paris, 1937
Competition entry
1936

1922

USSR Pavilion for the International Exposition in Paris, 1937
Competition entry
1936

Ada Fortunati
Cristina Meregalli
Scale 1:100

This was Melnikov's final project before the decades of oblivion that followed. The hard times had already begun: The project was developed during a well-orchestrated campaign against him in the Soviet media. The intention was to represent the USSR face-to-face with Nazi Germany's pavilion by Albert Speer, with both long structures standing symmetrically along the Seine, opposite the Eiffel Tower. One critic noted the structure's apparent instability: "like a steamship on the slipway – knock out a single wedge (as Charlie Chaplin does in *Modern Times*), and the whole mass would slide into the Seine."[1] A dramatic sequence of giant arches and cup-like forms – symbols of the Soviet republics and their capitals – created the entrance zone and led visitors inside, through dark interiors on the lower level to sunlit upper halls, creating a striking pupil-dilating effect. In the end, Boris Iofan's monumental pavilion was realized instead, serving as an enormous pedestal for Vera Mukhina's *Worker and Kolkhoz Woman* sculpture.

1 Yakov Kornfeld, "Projects of Soviet Pavilion for Paris International Exposition 1937," *Arkhitekturnaya Gazeta* [Architecture Newspaper], annex to no. 33 (1936), 4.

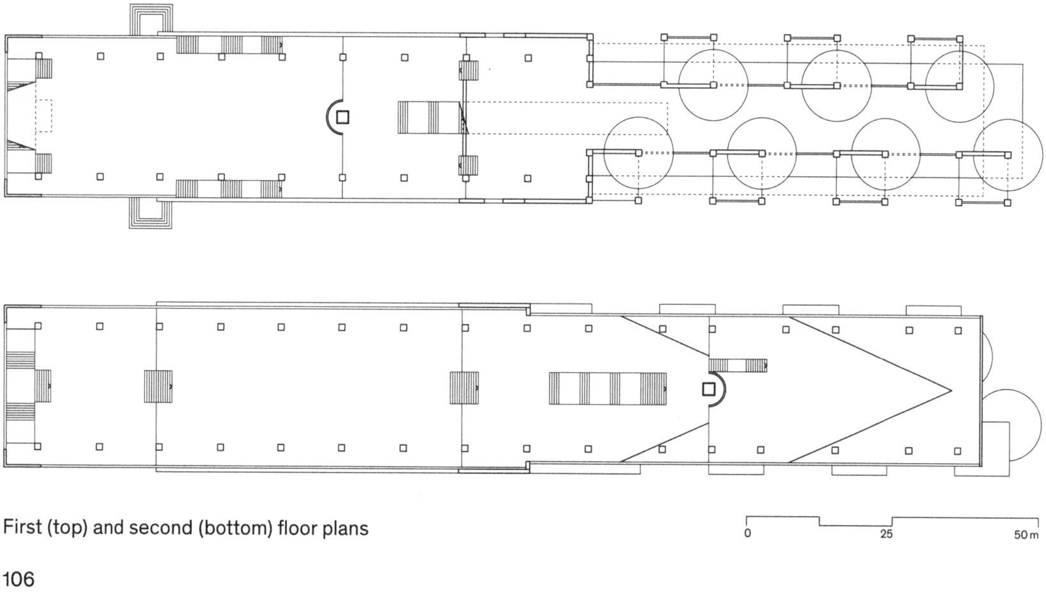

First (top) and second (bottom) floor plans

UNION
MOCKBA

USSR Pavilion for the World's Fair in New York, 1964 Competition entry 1962

Kyrre Beck Myreng
Lucia Prieto Heras
Scale 1:100

After decades of obscurity and silence, Melnikov sought to design his third USSR national pavilion – after Paris 1925 and 1937 – in New York. His motto, "The Shimmers of Celestial Mechanics," aimed to reflect the conquest of space. A mostly transparent, asymmetrical volume with a sharp diagonal axis rested on a rectangular base. Its curved roof of spatial triangles covered both interior halls and a vast open terrace. Melnikov emphasized the structure's division into upper and lower zones: "Top and bottom are spaced to the height of the cosmos … revealing hidden forces of celestial mechanics."[1] Escalators lifted visitors from modest ground-floor halls to a breath-taking 18-meter-high ceremonial hall. Despite all the differences from his early Makhorka pavilion (1923), the same choreographed journey remained: The open staircase served not as an entrance, but as a stage for the visitors' triumphant exit.

New Freedom, 1962–1974

Melnikov's design for the pavilion in New York is dated 1962, three years before his de facto rehabilitation. The Soviet leader Khrushchev publicly condemned him during this time: "Rusakov Club, designed by Comrade Melnikov, is an ugly, uncomfortable structure that looks like hell!"[2] The New York project opened Melnikov's New Freedom period: a brief return to architectural and public life in the 1960s, when he infused the common language of modernism with his personal architectural handwriting.

As well as the New York pavilion, this period includes his 1967 competition entry for a children's cinema on Arbat Street in Moscow. Its striking look was defined by a grand staircase slicing diagonally across the street facade and a 10-meter glass sphere, filled with light and air, that enclosed a spiral staircase and linked the large and small rectangular screening halls.

The New Freedom period was not only about new designs but also about writing his major text, *Architecture of My Life* – a poetic and naïve autobiography, a confession of love to his goddess, Architecture, and a reflectio on the role of the architect. Unable to publish this work in the USSR, he sought other ways t share his legacy – through teaching and by welcoming a stream of architectural pilgrims to his house on Krivoarbatsky Lane.

Hoping to break through his isolation, he corre-sponded intensively with a publishing house in Prague. Later he hosted two young America scholars: Arthur Sprague (Columbia University, 1965) and Frederick Starr (Princeton Univer-sity, 1967). He maintained warm relations with both, and in 1978 Starr, with the help of Sprague's materials, published the world's first monograph on Melnikov. Other figures who helped bring his name back into the internationa public eye included the *New York Times* architecture critic Ada Louise Huxtable and the Magnum photographers Henri Cartier-Bresson and Martine Franck.

1 Konstantin Melnikov, "Explanatory note to the project of USSR Pavilion for World's Fair in New York," Melnikov House archive, inv. 1043 (1962), 41.
2 *Izvestiia*, March 10, 1963, no. 59, 3.

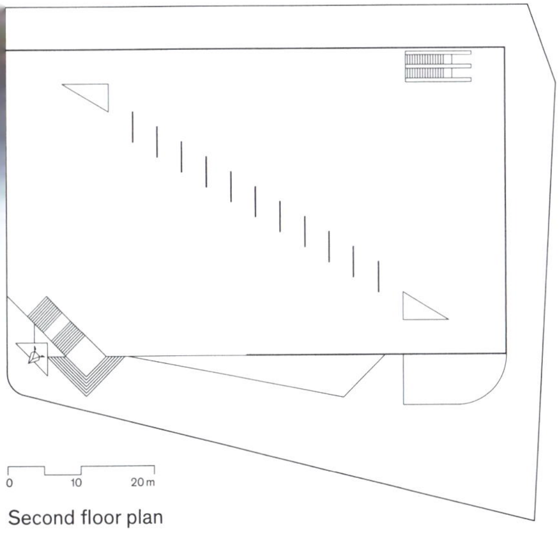

Second floor plan

USSR Pavilion for the World's Fair
in New York, 1964
Competition entry
1962

Melnikov: Architect of the Impossible

Pavel Kuznetsov

In the spring of 1925, two promising young architects – Charles-Édouard Jeanneret (later known as Le Corbusier) and Konstantin Melnikov – met at the International Exposition in Paris. The unusual pavilions they designed stood literally around the corner from each other near the Grand Palais, surrounded by the traditional palace-like pavilions of other countries – enough to provoke scandals in the press. They became acquainted, but afterward their paths diverged forever. Within a few years, each produced a masterpiece of residential design: Le Corbusier with the Villa Savoye outside Paris, and Melnikov with his cylindrical house-studio in Moscow. We know a great deal about Le Corbusier – his legacy fills entire library shelves – but what about Melnikov?

Who Are You, Mr. Melnikov?

The life of Konstantin Stepanovich Melnikov (1890–1974), one of the most controversial architects of modernism, in many ways reflects the tragic history of Russia in the twentieth century. A talented boy from the lower social classes before the revolution, he received a brilliant education as an artist and architect. His talent, recognized early on and nurtured by a philanthropist, would, twenty years later, bring him the applause of heads of state in Paris, where he achieved global recognition for his design of the USSR Pavilion in 1925.

The Russian Revolution of 1917 became Melnikov's second social "lift." Numerous competition entries and his first implemented projects brought him closer to the intellectuals among the Bolshevik elite. His projects were exhibited in Warsaw, New York, Madrid and Milan. However, with the onset of Stalin's cultural revolution in the 1930s, Melnikov's refusal to compromise his own creative principles led to bullying, isolation and a ban on the architecture profession. His meteoric career ended when he was just forty-eight, followed by decades marked by oblivion, obscurity and the struggle to survive. In the late 1920s he had been a prolific practitioner, juggling a dozen projects at once, yet he saw none of his designs realized in the second half of his life.

Rehabilitation and later recognition came only in the 1960s, shortly before his death. Although the architect's main works are public and industrial buildings (workers' clubs, exhibition pavilions, garages), perhaps his most famous building is his own house-studio in Moscow, composed of two interlocking cylinders.

Melnikov was decades ahead of his time and its technical possibilities. For his projects, he chose shapes that were inconvenient, forms that architects tend to avoid – the triangle, parallelogram, diagonal, cone, pyramid, saw and spiral. He was an experimenter, although none of his workers' club buildings were embodied as the author envisioned. His architecture was transformable, dynamic and in several projects even kinetic. And it was always "speaking," with expressive, strikingly memorable forms. Melnikov never rejected either tradition or innovation. His avant-garde oeuvre absorbed the traditions of Russian architecture of the past and would go on to influence the world of architectural thought of the twenty-first century.

Melnikov proudly inscribed not the name of Lenin or Stalin, but his own name and profession on the facade of his house in 1929. A "solo architect in a mass society" – this is how his first biographer, S. Frederick Starr[1], described Melnikov.

Melnikov's System: Architecture Beyond Architecture

Often considered a utopianist, Melnikov emphasized in his texts and conversations that one-third of his designs were realized – enough to be considered not just a paper architect but a real practitioner. In numbers, this means that nineteen of his fifty-five projects were actually built, although only thirteen have survived to the present day. This is mostly due to the temporary nature of structures such as exhibition pavilions.

He was one of those architects who did not hesitate to enter alien territory – be it mechanical structures, technological processes or solutions for transport and logistics. His innovations pertained to much more than just architecture. Melnikov's oeuvre was "mega-architecture": essentially an expression of his ideas, whether philosophical, technological or artistic.

He constantly proposed his own system – "Melnikov's System," as he called it – in such diverse areas as residential house-communes, car parking, communal recreation and resorts and more, offering a comprehensive recipe that surpassed the limits of architecture per se and entered into the domains of production, movement, housing and human rehabilitation.

For example, rather than designing the traditional buildings expected for the Green City resort (1930), Melnikov proposed something more ambitious: a system for rationalized sleep and recuperation. This led him to create a series of "sleeping sonata" buildings. A year earlier, he had designed a "golden bedroom," or temple of sleep, for his own family. Both projects were inspired by Melnikov's theory of sleep, which was not strictly scientific but deeply spiritual: During the day a person gets tired and ages, but at night during sleep they recover strength and are rejuvenated. Each morning they are reborn.

He later wrote: "A human being sleeps for a third of his or her life. If we take a sixty-year life span, then sleep accounts for twenty years: twenty years of unconscious, unguided voyages through enigmatic worlds into the unknown depths serving as sources of salutary mysteries and even miracles – yes, perhaps even miracles."[2]

The sources of Melnikov's views on the role of sleep were, on the one hand, the religious philosophy of Russian Cosmism by Nikolai Fedorov (1829–1903), with its idea of physically overcoming death. On the other hand, they drew from the ideas – widespread among some Bolshevik intellectual elites of the 1920s – that progress in the life sciences and experimental visionary biology could bring humanity closer to immortality.

His proposal for the Green City sparked debate and, as one might expect, did not win the competition. From today's perspective – amid the rising popularity of biohacking and ongoing efforts to improve quality (and even the duration) of life through scientifically based practices – Melnikov's sleep laboratories of the 1920s can be seen as an early approach to mastering sleep as a tool that humans could use more efficiently and purposefully.

For the seven workers' clubs he was commissioned to design by regional trade unions from 1927 to 1930, instead of "normal" buildings he proposed something his clients had not expected: a "Melnikov system of halls" to transform the clubs' interiors, similar to the manipulations of a Rubik's Cube. For him, the very concept of the workers' club implied multifunctionality, as opposed to using the space solely as a large assembly or auditorium hall. The variety of club rooms – differing in both size and function – and the possibility of combining them naturally led to spatial transformation: With movable walls and floors, spaces could contract and expand, becoming large theaters or cinemas, small classrooms, hobby rooms, sports halls or even swimming pools. Unfortunately, Melnikov's vision outstripped the engineering capabilities and available technologies of his time. In practice, the "living" walls were functional for only a brief period, and only in one of the six clubs that were ultimately built – the Rusakov Club.

All his projects are a manifesto of architecture "on the edge of the possible" and even beyond it – an attempt by the author to prove, first to himself, that it is both possible and necessary to be independent of fashionable new building materials and engineers, and that avant-garde designs can be achieved with simple, traditional means and technologies. These projects embody the eternal dream of architects to free themselves from the dominance of engineers and builders, to work without dependence on any particular material – whether concrete, plastic or composites. It was the realization of Occam's razor in architecture: Do not multiply complexity beyond what is necessary; if it can be done simply, do it simply.

Melnikov's universal value today lies not only in his individual projects, but above all in his approach to architecture as an art "at its limits" and in his persistent efforts to push those limits using straightforward, "unfashionable" technologies and materials.

Architecture as an Art: Form or Function?

Although the "golden age" of Melnikov's work – 1925 to 1931 – coincided with the heyday of Soviet Constructivism, the architect was offended when he was called a Constructivist. The leaders of that movement – Moisei Ginzburg and the Vesnin brothers – were Melnikov's most important creative opponents. They were followers of the functionalist ideas of Le Corbusier (whom Melnikov also couldn't stand, their 1925 meeting in Paris notwithstanding) in Soviet Russia. For the Constructivists, the function and structures of architecture were paramount, while for Melnikov the priority was form and beauty. He understood architecture as an art.

Indeed, his house of two cylinders intersecting by one-third of their volume is a pure, entirely independent "sculptural" form. It could be imagined in any landscape, not necessarily in the city – in the desert, on the seacoast or in the woods.

"Architecture is not about expediency. Architecture is Beauty – there is no other, there has never been and there never will be."[3] Melnikov's fellows – Soviet Rationalists from the ASNOVA movement led by Nikolai Ladovsky – emphasized the role of architectural form and its influence on the human psyche, highlighting the mind's perception of architectural imagery. But unlike Ladovsky, who tried to introduce a scientific approach into architectural design (even launching a psychotechnical laboratory at VKhUTEMAS), for Melnikov the focus on the perception of architectural form was intuitive. The birth of architectural design was for him a purely artistic act that could not be rationalized or even explained.

This is why he taught for years but was never successful in creating a school of followers. He was always a solo architect, even while working as the head of one of the architecture studios under the Moscow City Council. Throughout his life, he was always afraid of repeating others and even tried to avoid self-plagiarism. His projects – both built and unrealized – are instantly memorable, leaving a lasting imprint on the mind.

For Melnikov, designing form always came first, ahead of function. One of the best examples of this is his project for the Zuev Workers' Club, a public building for hundreds of visitors. He conceived it as a chain of five interlocking cylinders but lost the closed competition to his friend Ilya Golosov in March 1927. One month later, the same formal idea of interlocking cylinders was reborn in the layout of his house-studio, a modest structure for four inhabitants – completely different functionally from the club. Functional spaces were then built within the chosen form. This does not mean he ignored functionality – the causality was two-way – but looking at the incredibly diverse floor plans and geometric solids he employed, the role of form appears dominant.

"My tools of architectural luxury were its elegant servants:
Symmetry beyond symmetry
The boundless elasticity of the diagonal
The full-bodied slenderness of the triangle
The ethereal weight of the console"[4]

Tradition and Modernism

He never considered the old and new as in opposition to each other, writing once: "Classics and modern are two architectural horses."[5] This is another fundamental difference from the Constructivists, who worked "from scratch," denying the past and inventing, like medieval alchemists, dozens of new low-cost building materials – xylolite, kamyshyt, fibrolite, hollow concrete stones.

In his early avant-garde architecture (1922–1927), Melnikov employed entirely traditional building materials: brick, wood, glass and plaster – practically no concrete – and chalk paints based on natural pigments. Yet the projects were truly experimental in terms of the interplay of spaces and structural decisions. One can strive to reach the heights of architecture using entirely simple, "poor" materials. In the words of his creative opponent, Le Corbusier: "Le grand art vit de moyens pauvre."[6]

Catherine Cooke, a pioneering scholar of early Soviet modernism, defined Melnikov's approach as "low-tech" in comparison to the "high-tech" approach of his Soviet Constructivist contemporaries (M. Ginzburg, A. Vesnin and others).[7] The Makhorka and Paris exhibition pavilions, as well as his house-studio, are perfect examples of low-tech avant-garde human-scale structures with well-thought-out visual connections. They grew out of the traditional building culture and techniques of former Russia: They were built according to the norms of Count de Rochefort's *Urochnoe polozhenie*,[8] the main building standard in Russia in the nineteenth and early twentieth centuries.

Melnikov himself originated from a peasant, deeply Orthodox, spiritual culture. From 1905 to 1917, he received an excellent "old school" education as an artist and architect. He was a person from ancient regime.

It is no coincidence that in the 1920s he positioned both the office building of the New Sukharev Market and his own house on their assigned lots in such a way as to ensure not only optimal insolation and other practical benefits, but also framed views of the era's urban dominants: churches. Even his workers' clubs – a new typology promoted by the Soviet authorities as an ideological alternative to the Orthodox Church – such as the Kauchuk and Dulevo Clubs, do not confront the nearby churches but instead coexist with them in a surprisingly harmonious manner.

Clients and Patrons

A widespread but simplistic assumption holds that after the Russian Revolution of 1917 – with private ownership abolished and private commissions gone – the Soviet state became the sole client for architects. In reality, the state and its elite were far from homogeneous. In the 1920s and 1930s, in the absence of private patrons, the true "clients" included not only public institutions but also the individuals who represented them at every stage – from programming to design to implementation.

Konstantin Melnikov, among the most prolific architects of the era, offers an exemplary case study of this dynamic. His career reveals the complex interplay between architect and client body, whose actors ranged from central and regional authorities to trade unions and high-ranking party functionaries.

Some of his patrons, such as People's Commissar and ambassador Leonid Krasin (1924–1926), are easily identifiable. Others, less well known but no less important, included Ilya Tsivtsivadze (1927–1931), Juvenal Slavinsky (1931–1933) and Ivan Mezhlauk (1934–1936), all of whom maintained long-term professional relationships with Melnikov. Members of the Soviet political elite, from the People's Commissar for Finance to the head of the Uzbekistan government and the mayor of Moscow, were guests at his home. These alliances – between officials seeking politically significant architectural projects and a young, talented architect – proved mutually beneficial.

Melnikov's relationships with his clients defy easy categorization. Some were collaborative, granting him complete creative freedom, as with the Paris pavilion project (1925) or the trade unions that embraced his transformable designs and unconventional club architecture. Others were rooted in personal patronage, as in the Makhorka project (1923), where political support enabled him to implement a revolutionary vertical production layout against the original wishes of the institutional client, the All-Russian Tobacco Syndicate. Many relationships were marked by difficult negotiations over budgets, materials and technological limitations, as in the case of the bus and truck garages for Moscow City Communal Services (1926–1928).

What stands out is Melnikov's proactive approach to design and programming: He rarely accepted a brief as given, but expanded, reframed or transformed it into something far beyond the client's original vision. His career forms a vivid case study in how an architect of extraordinary talent navigated – and ultimately failed to navigate – the layered, shifting network of Soviet "clients" in an era without private commissions. Even under a centralized, authoritarian system, architecture was shaped by the dynamics between individuals: the architect's vision, the client's ambitions and the political and economic constraints of the time.

Melnikov's recently discovered diaries reveal not an untouchable icon, but a living, contradictory figure – a man of his epoch, struggling to survive, to negotiate and to find consensus with the state.

A Non-Soviet Man

He was never truly a Soviet man – yet neither was he a dissident or an anti-Soviet person. The word that best describes him is *non-Soviet*. He served the regime as an architect only to the extent necessary to obtain commissions – from the sarcophagus for Lenin's body to the Soviet exhibition pavilions – for architects are inherently opportunistic, dependent on resources, that is, on a client, to bring their visions to life. Yet in his heart, Melnikov remained deeply religious and profoundly apart from Soviet ideology, as his diaries clearly reveal. Across the twentieth century, he succeeded in creating and maintaining a small non-Soviet universe – a private microcosm within his cylindrical house in the heart of the Soviet capital. This was more than a family home: It was his sanctuary, his creative laboratory and a treasury with his archive. A sincere believer, even in the years of aggressive state atheism in the USSR, he put a kiot with icons in the most prominent place in his house.

Nevertheless, from the very beginning, he was cursed within the Soviet system. The fact that he wrote his name and profession in big concrete-made letters on the street facade of his house in 1927 shows how far removed from political reality he was: It was like a time bomb that exploded ten years later, during the public campaign against the "formalism" of the intelligentsia. At that time, he found himself sharing the fate of composer Dmitri Shostakovich, artist Vladimir Lebedev and many other victims of the Stalinist regime. When he was dismissed from teaching at the Architecture Institute in March 1936 for "refusal to revise his creative position,"[9] it was exactly the truth, because he could not pretend or imitate Classicist models of the past: "I could never design anything that might invite boredom. To me, anything that resembled something already seen seemed uninteresting and dull."[10]

He was modest, not arrogant, and unassuming in daily life, but he always knew his own value and was proud to be part of the profession. Much later, in 1967, he wrote: "Do you think I consider myself a genius? No, I'm an architect – it's the same thing ... True creativity exists only where one can say, 'This is my own.' ... For me, speaking about architecture is, in essence, speaking about myself."[11]

The case of Melnikov is especially relevant today, in a time of growing neo-totalitarian regimes. It allows us to understand the roots of inhuman systems from the moment they are born and trace their evolution, as well as the technologies of oppression used against talented individuals within them. The relationship of artists with authorities under dictatorship is something that many creative people continue to struggle with. If creativity could find its way in the 1920s and 1930s, is there still room for it in today's authoritarian regimes?

1 S. Frederick Starr, *Melnikov: Solo Architect in a Mass Society* (Princeton, New Jersey: Princeton University Press, 1978).
2 Konstantin Melnikov, "*Architecture of My Life,*" manuscript, Melnikov House archive, inv. 1060 (1967).
3 Ibid.
4 Ibid.
5 K. Melnikov's maxim, written in charcoal, is displayed on a panel in the living room of the architect's house in Moscow. Melnikov House archive, inv. 389.
6 Le Corbusier, *L'Art décoratif d'aujourd'hui* (Paris: Editions Crès, 1925).
7 Catherine Cooke, *Russian Avant-Garde: Theories of Art, Architecture and the City* (London: Academy Editions, 1995), 136.
8 N. I. de Rochefort, *Illyustrirovannoe urochnoe polozhenie* [Illustrated work regulation: Manual for drawing up, verifying estimates, designing and executing works] (Petrograd: Publishing House of K. L. Ricker, 1918).
9 Directive No. 43 issued by the Architecture Institute, Melnikov House archive, inv. 396/139 (March 1936), 14.
10 Konstantin Melnikov, "Construction and Architect," in: *Architectural Composition: Contemporary Issues* (Moscow, 1970), 20–23.
11 Konstantin Melnikov, "Architecture of My Life," manuscript, Melnikov House archive, inv. 1060 (1967).

Situating Melnikov

To understand Melnikov, one must first situate him within the world of his contemporaries. The four cases highlighted on the following pages – Nikolai Ladovsky (1881–1941), El Lissitzky (1890–1941), Ivan Leonidov (1902–1959) and Georgy Krutikov (1899–1958) – could easily be expanded to dozens more. These avant-garde heroes came from provincial towns, often from small villages. The older generation (Ladovsky and Melnikov himself) received a traditional "old school" education before 1917. Many others, such as El Lissitzky, were constrained by the Pale of Settlement in Tsarist Russia and compelled to study in Europe. It was the Revolution that opened a fast track and a window of opportunity for them.

This first wave of the avant-garde created a school with an almost magical name, VKhUTEMAS, where they, along with colleagues such as Alexander Vesnin, Moisei Ginzburg, Alexander Rodchenko, Vladimir Tatlin and many others, taught and experimented with students – and sometimes on them. They nurtured a second generation, one perhaps even freer and more daring than themselves, including Leonidov and Krutikov, who also went on to teach and inspire. Everything came to an end in the early 1930s when Stalin's cultural policies dissolved the Constructivists, Rationalists and other avant-garde movements. Yet the long and painful death of Soviet avant-garde architecture dragged on into the second half of the decade.

These architects built only a fraction of what they imagined: Leonidov, for instance, became known as "the architect of one staircase" (in reference to the park steps at the Ordzhonikidze Sanatorium in Kislovodsk). For this reason, the paper legacy of unrealized projects – in sketches, drawings and texts – is just as important as the architecture that was actually completed.

Ivan Leonidov
Lenin Institute for Librarianship
VKhUTEMAS diploma project
Moscow, 1927

Mara Mari
Francisco Silva
Scale 1:200

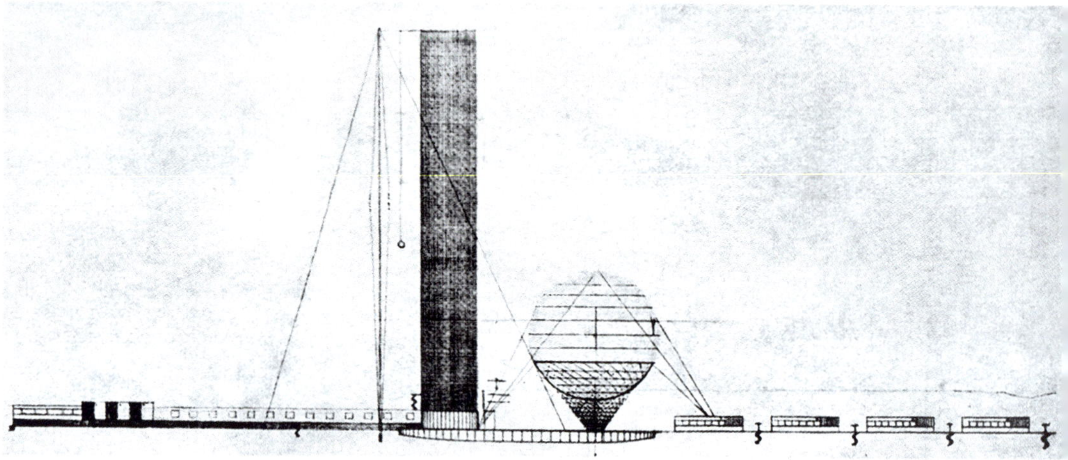

Elevation

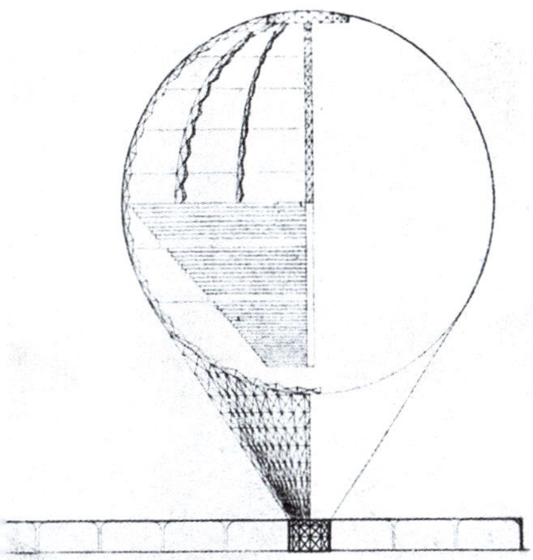

Section of the auditorium

Ivan Leonido, who belonged to a younger generation of Soviet avant-gardists than Melnikov and Ladovsky, was condemned and effectively banned almost from his student years. A special term was even coined to discredit him: *leonidovschina*, or Leonidovism.

Leonidov rejected Melnikov's concept of the workers' club as a single transformable building – an architectural Rubik's Cube – and instead envisioned these structures as spatial compositions of freestanding (or rather free-floating) cosmic forms in open landscapes: pyramids, paraboloids, masts and more.

His diploma project, the Lenin Institute for Librarianship, is a composition of three spatial axes that seemingly float on the slope of Sparrow Hills. A giant semiglazed, convertible spherical auditorium with 4,000 seats barely touches the circular platform of the science theater; held in place by steel cables, it resembles a hot-air balloon ready for takeoff. A 150-meter parallelepiped tower houses 15 million books which can be distributed via conveyors to three different horizontal blocks: the reading rooms, Institute for Library Science, and research laboratories. A radio antenna and "aerotram" represent new technologies of communication and connection.

Like Melnikov, Leonidov came from a peasant background. Unsurprisingly, his deep-rooted sense of the vastness of Russian space found expression in cosmic designs that embraced openness rather than dense urban fabric. What united him with Melnikov was a shared belief in architecture not merely as construction, but as a tool for shaping a new society.

Georgy Krutikov
The Flying City
VKhUTEIN diploma project
1928

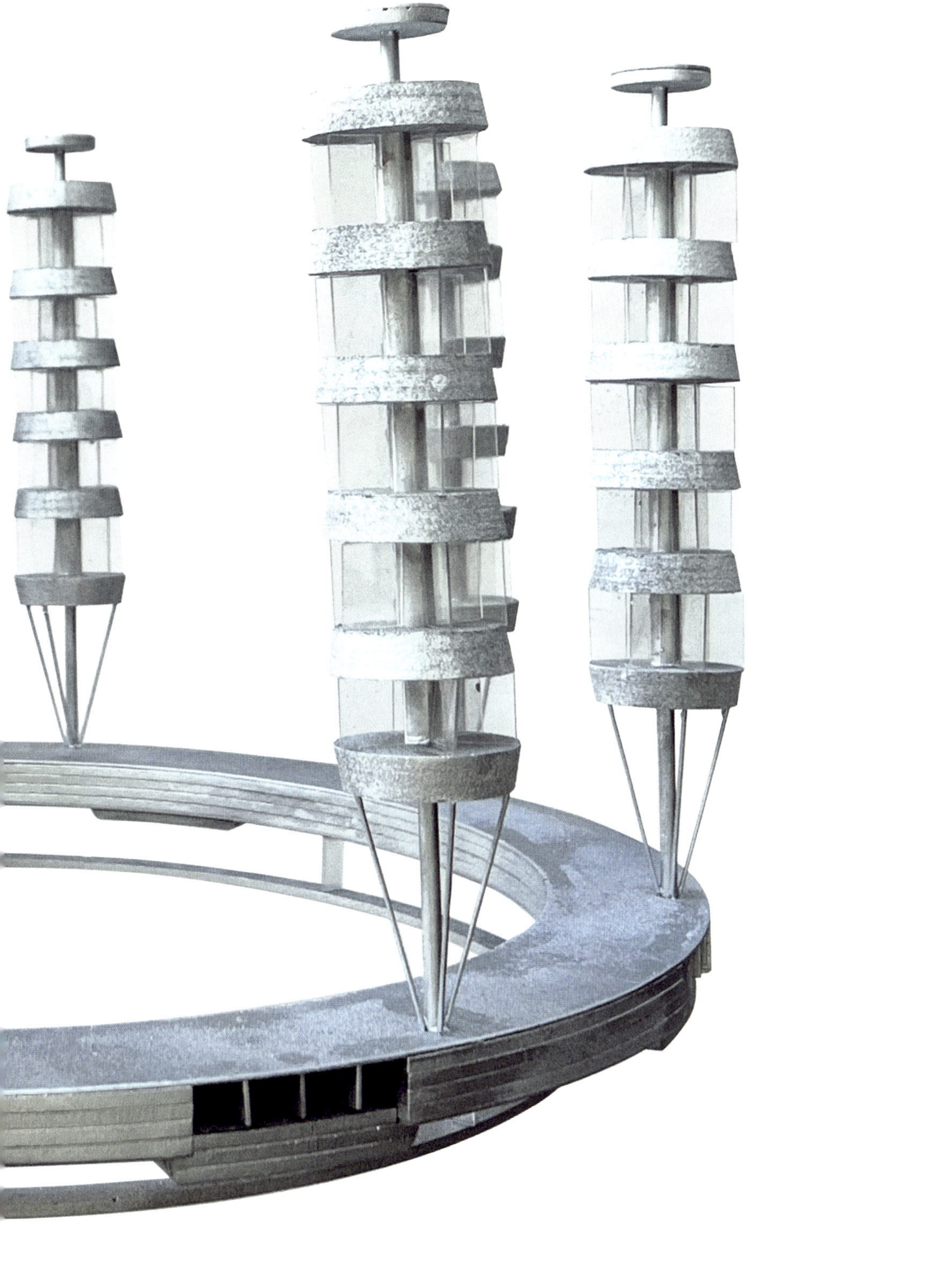

Georgy Krutikov
The Flying City
VKhUTEIN diploma project
1928

Matilde Caviglia
Jens Rudolf Ugelstad
Scale 1:200

Georgy Krutikov, a student of Ladovsky's and his right hand at the psychotechnical laboratory, explored the idea of motion in architecture in a radically different way from Melnikov's kinetic projects – the Columbus monument-lighthouse, Leningrad Pravda and MOSPS Theater. Krutikov titled his 1928 diploma project at VKhUTEMAS (which was called VKhUTEIN at the time) City on Air Routes. Better known today as the Flying City, it imagined daily home-to-work commuting between cosmic space and Earth. In the analytical part he studied the evolution of mobile forms, means of transportation and early mobile dwellings. The project itself described in detail residential complexes of house-communes hovering in near space. Futuristic egg-shaped flying cabins would shuttle the residents to working zones on Earth. Each of the three collective dwelling types that Krutikov designed includes a developed communal block (canteen, club, gym), visible in the drawings as a ring uniting vertical clusters of residential units, and a docking bay for flying cabins.

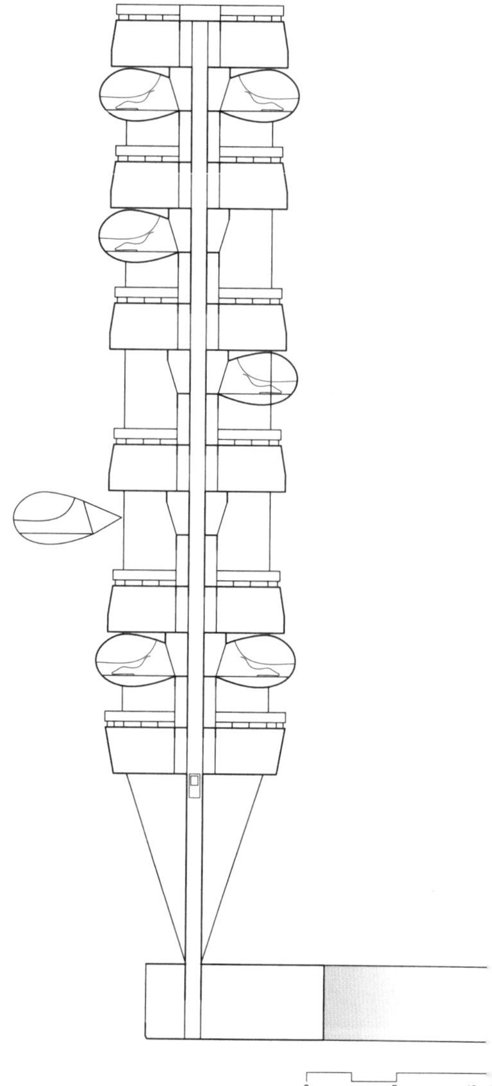

Section of a house-commune with docking bays for mobile capsules

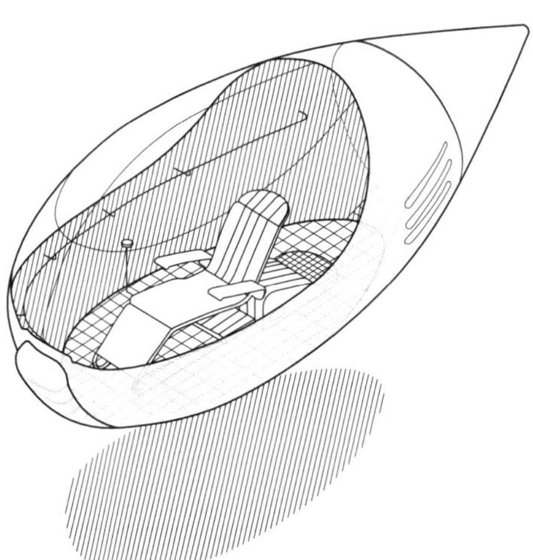

General view of a mobile capsule, imagined as a universal means of transportation

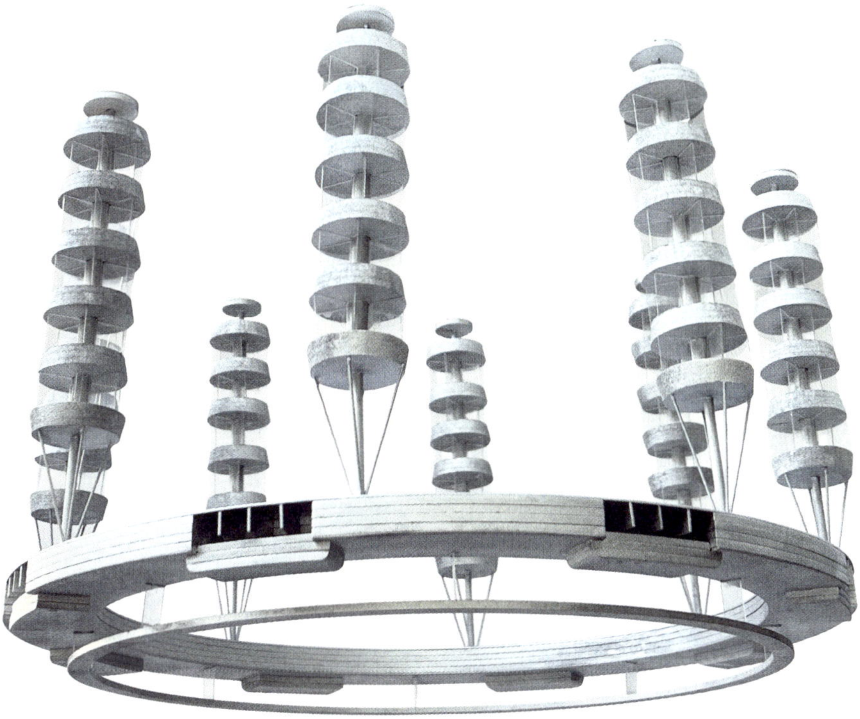

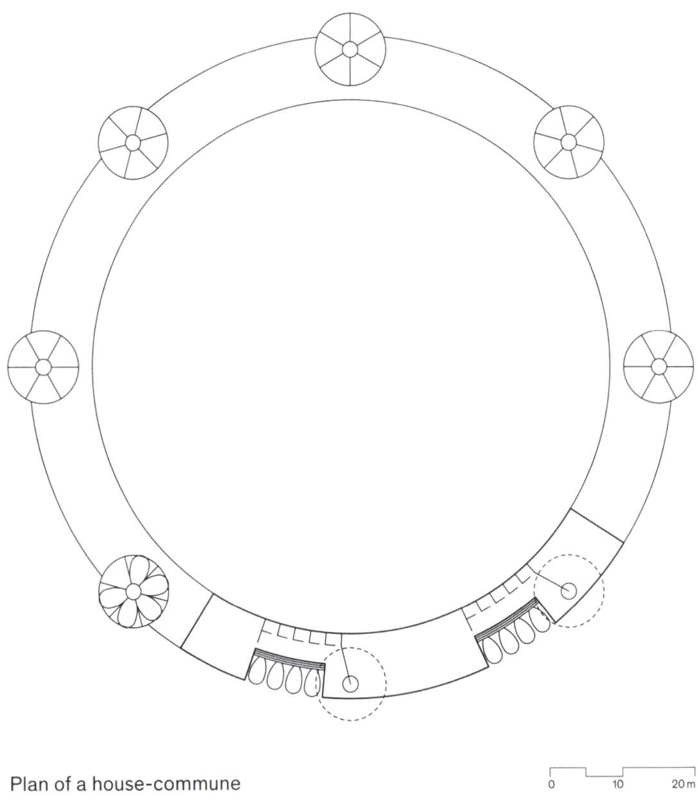

Plan of a house-commune

0 10 20 m

Nikolai Ladovsky
Columbus Monument-Lighthouse
Competition entry
Santo Domingo, Dominican Republic, 1929

Gregory Benoit
Scale 1:200

Perspective of the Columbus monument

Nikolai Ladovsky's proposal for the monument-lighthouse was not fully appreciated by the international jury, much like the kinetic project by his colleague Melnikov. The winning design was a lying Latin cross by the then twenty-two-year-old Scotsman J. L. Gleave.

One of the most avant-garde entries in the competition, along with that of the Soviet Constructivist Ivan Leonidov, Ladovsky's cross-shaped skyscraper by the ocean metaphorically alludes more to the conquest of space than to the literal celebration of America's discovery by the great Genoese explorer. The alternating pattern of opaque and semi-transparent sections creates a magnetic formal rhythm, inviting future Spider-Men to scale its heights and accomplish feats for humanity comparable to Columbus's remarkable endeavor.

Melnikov's competition entry for the same project, see pages 74–75

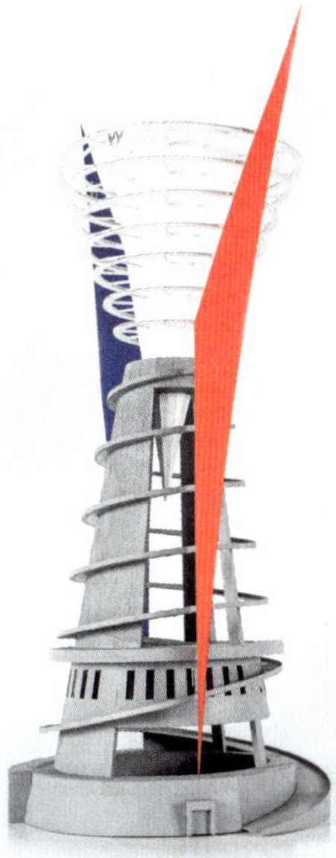

El Lissitzky
Wolkenbügel
(Horizontal Skyscraper for Moscow)
Unbuilt project
1924–1925

Elena Robatto
Mario Poma
Scale 1:100

The Soviet Rationalist organization ASNOVA (Association of the New Architects) published only one bulletin, in June 1926. It included a programmatic text by Nikolai Ladovsky on the foundations of architectural theory and a description of El Lissitzky's visionary Wolkenbügel (WB) project – a horizontal skyscraper, in contrast to the vertical American type.

The greatest challenge the WB posed to the public was psychological: to comprehend a massive horizontal structure suspended in the air, supported by three semitransparent legs.

More urbanistic than purely architectural, the WB was revolutionary in its context. One need only look at photos of mid-1920s Moscow to imagine its potential impact. Replicable and low-cost, the eight planned WB structures, each 50 meters high, could have radically transformed the city's traditional low-rise skyline. Also forward-thinking was the WB's integration with public transit: Tram stops were planned at the base of two legs, with a metro entrance built into the third – visionary given that the first subway line would not open until 1935.

In the text on the WB, El Lissitzky thanked his Swiss colleague Emil Roth, who brought Lissitzky's sky-high ideas down to earth, converting them from paper architecture into buildable projects with engineering calculations. Initially consulting on structures, Roth ultimately influenced significant changes to the entire project.

At the end of his article, Lissitzky announced an alternative version of the Wolkenbügel – WB2. While never published, WB2 is known from a few surviving sketches: an oblique form of three crossed inclined legs, reminiscent of Tatlin Tower (1919).

Pietro Borzacca
Francesco Tucci
Scale: 1:10,000

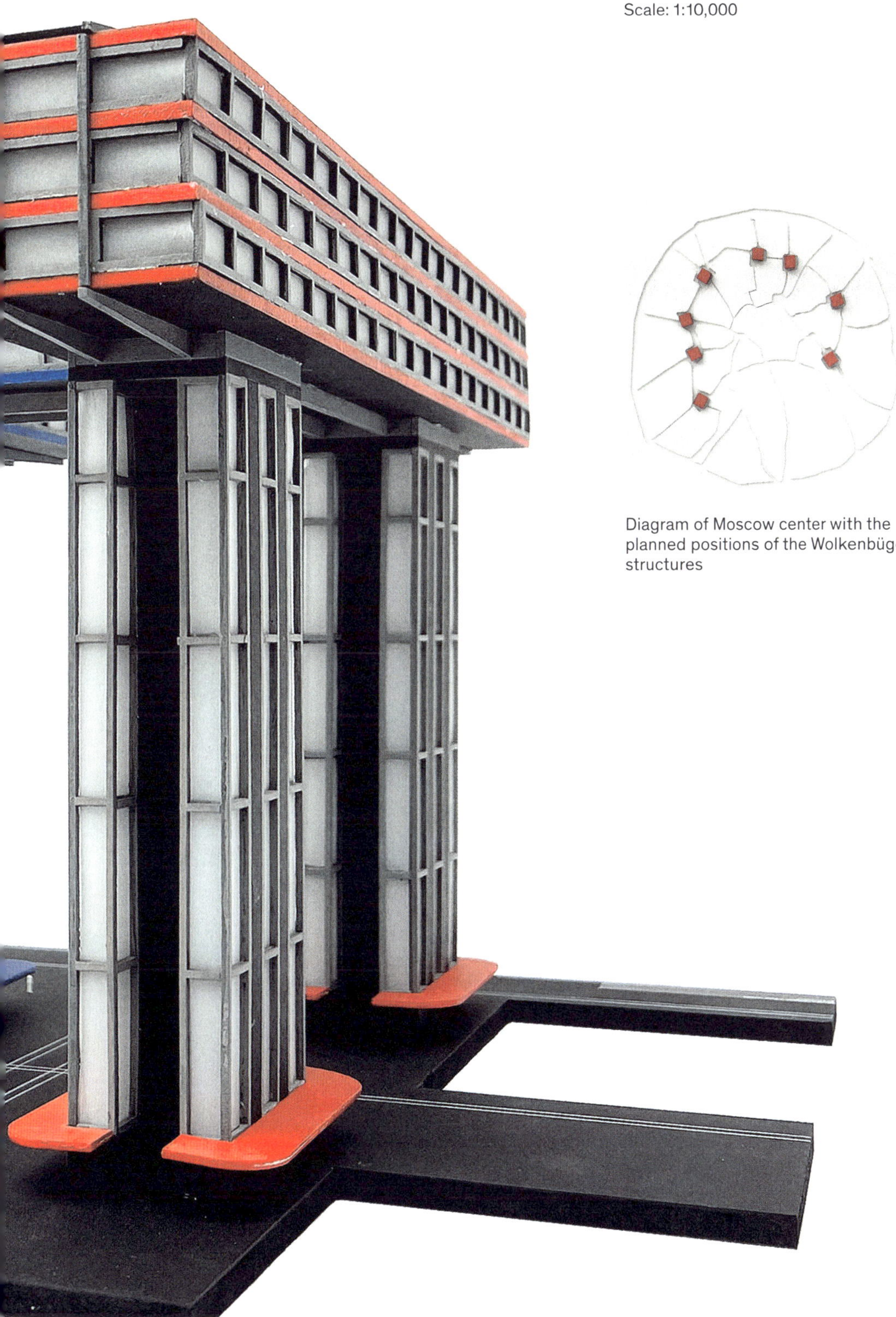

Diagram of Moscow center with the planned positions of the Wolkenbügel structures

ASNOVA Bulletin, Moscow, 1926

What united El Lissitzky with the Soviet Rationalists was their shared concern with the perception of architecture. The experience of seeing Lissitzky's Wolkenbügel (WB) while moving toward or away from the Kremlin or along the Boulevard Ring reflected Nikolai Ladovsky's principle of *ratio-architecture*: not only *technical rationality* (economy of materials and labor), but also *architectural rationality* – the economy of psychic energy required to perceive the spatial and functional aspects of a structure.

The Rationalist ASNOVA association, which was opposed to the functionalist OSA (an organization of Soviet Constructivists), introduced applied psychology into architectural practice. In the bulletin Ladovsky announced the establishment of a psychotechnical laboratory at VKhUTEMAS that would extend Hugo Münsterberg's experiments at Harvard to architecture.

For the Rationalists, color was one of the key tools for shaping the perception of architecture. In the WB, El Lissitzky used a red and blue color scheme to help Muscovites to navigate. His color-marking facades correspond to other experimental practices of the time, such as Melnikov's "sea of architectural painting" for guiding people through the rows of a thousand kiosks at the New Sukharev Market (1925), Hinnerk Scheper's interior orientation for the Narkomfin building (1929–1930) and ASNOVA's color schemes for the housing blocks of the Khavsko-Shabolovsky district (Travin, Josephovich et al., 1927–1930).

In the bulletin, ASNOVA also proposed to the Moscow City Council a system of street painting designed to unify facades rather than highlight individual buildings.

Following pages:
The ASNOVA bulletin in its entirety

НЕПЕРИОДИЧЕСКОЕ ИЗДАНИЕ

ACS

АСНОВА

HNOOBW A

ИЗВЕСТИЯ АССОЦИАЦИИ НОВЫХ АРХИТЕКТОРОВ
MITTEILUNGEN DER ASSOTIATION NEUER ARCHITEKTEN
REVUE DE L'ASOTIATION D'ARCHITECTES CONTEMPORAINE

Д РЕДАКЦИЕЙ: ЭЛЬ ЛИСИЦКОГО—Н. А. ЛАДОВСКОГО■REDAKTION: EL LISSITZKY—N. A. LADOWSKY

МОСКВА, Мясницкая 21, кв. 35. тел. 4-95-75
MOSKAU. Mjasnitzkaja 21, w. 35. tel. 4-95-75
MOSCOU. Miasnizkaia 21, at 35. tel. 4-95-75

1926 1926 1926 1926 1926 1926 1926 1926 1926 1926 1926 1926 1926 1296 1926 1926 1926 1926 1926 1926 1926 1926 1926 1926 1926 1926

АСНОВА

1926

A S N O W A

ССР — **С**троитель нового бытия.

СССР — **С**обиратель классовой энергии для построения бесклассового общества.

СССР — **С**тавит новые задачи так-же и архитектуре.

СССР — **Р**ационализованный труд в единстве с наукой и высоко развитой техникой.

СНОВА считает своей основой материальное воплощение в архитектуре принципов СССР.

СНОВА считает срочным вооружение архитектуры орудиями и методами современной науки.

СНОВА считает, что для продвижения современной архитектуры, сегодняшний стратегический момент требует взаимного созидательного труда архитекторов-производителей с одной стороны и трудящихся масс потребителей с другой. Сегодняшняя практическая работа завершится завтра в теоретической системе.

СНОВА исходя из темпа современного изобретательства, когда каждый день ставит архитектора перед новыми техническими организмами, считает, для данного положения, наиболее важным установление обобщающих принципов в архитектуре и освобождения ея от атрофирующихся форм.

СНОВА работает над созданием точных и научных терминов в современной архитектуре, считая их существенным орудием ея совершенствования.

ТОТ ЕЧАТНЫЙ ИСТ **АСНОВА** СТЬ:

1. Концентр декретирующих современную архитектуру.
2. Громкоговоритель строющих ее.
3. Оповеститель науки и техники современной архитектуры. (теории и практики).
4. Перекидывает мост для идущих к архитектуре из других областей пластических и технических искусств.
5. . . . .

ПРЕДСТАВИТЕЛИ ЗАГРАНИЦЕЙ: ГЕРМАНИЯ—АДОЛЬФ БЭНЕ■ФРАНЦИЯ—ЛЕ КОРБЮЗЬЕ■ГОЛАНДИЯ—МАРТ СТАМ■АМЕРИКА—ЛУНДБЕРГ ХОЛЬМ■ШВЕЙЦАРИЯ—ЭМИЛЬ РООТ■ЧЕХОСЛОВАКИЯ—КАРЕЛЬ ТЕЙГЕ■ЮГОСЛАВИЯ—ЛЮБОМИР МИЦИЧ■ЯПОНИЯ—МУРАЯМА

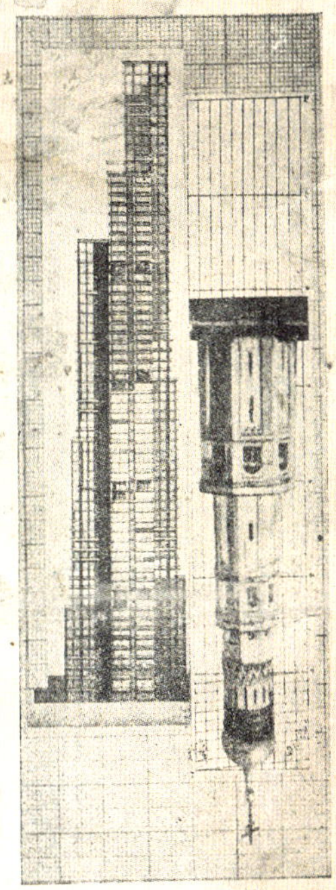

ДЛЯ КОГО РАБОТАЕТ АСНОВА?

АСНОВА работает для массы которая требует:

а. архитектуры однозначной, как автомобиль или сапог.

б. от жилья больше, чем только аппарат для отправления естественных нужд.

в. от архитектуры рационального обоснования качеств ея.

г. не дил[illegible]а, а мастерства.

КТО РАБОТАЕТ С АСНОВОЙ?

ВСЕ АРХИТЕКТОРА, сознающие свою ответственность за растущее строительство, которое грозит стать анархичным.

ВСЕ ИНЖЕНЕРЫ, стремящиеся к техническим сооружениям, стоящим на уровне искусства.

ВСЕ СТРОИТЕЛИ всего нового, пути которых пересекаются с архитектурой.

Серия небоскребов для Москвы. WB1 (1923—25)

Проект Эль Лисицкого

Вид сверху.

Предпосылки

Предлагаемый здесь новый тип постройки можно отнести к роду небоскребов. Он предназначается не для жилья, а для размещения центральных учреждений.

Тип высокого дома создала Америка превратив европейский горизонтальный корридор в вертикальную шахту лифта, вокруг которого нанизаны ярусы этажей. Рос этот тип совершенно анархично, без какой бы то ни было заботы об организации города в целом. Единственная его забота была перещеголять высотой и пышностью соседа.

При выработке нашего типа мы исходим из противоположных предпосылок:

1) Мы считаем, что часть подчиняется целому и система города определяет характер его сооружений

2) Мы говорим „сооружения“, а не „дома“, считая, что новый город должен преодолеть понятие индивидуального дома.

3) Мы считаем, что пока не изобретены возможности совершенно свободного парения, нам свойственней двигаться горизонтально, а не вертикально.

Поэтому, если для горизонтальной планировки на земле в данном участке нет места, мы подымаем требуемую полезную площадь на стойки и они служа комуникацией между горизонтальным тротуаром улиц и горизонтальным коридором сооружения. Цел максимум полезной площади при минимальной подпор Следствие: ясное членение функций.

Происхождение

Но есть-ли надобность строить в воздухе?

„Вообще“—нет. Пока есть еще достаточно мест на земле.

Но... „в частности“?

Мы живем в городах родившихся до нас. Темп и нуждам нашего дня они уже не удовлетворяют. М не можем сбрить их с сегодня на завтра и „правильно вновь выстроить. Невозможно сразу изменить и структуру и тип. Москва относится по своему план к концетрическому средневековому типу. (Париж Вена). Структура ея: центр — Кремль, кольцо А кольцо Б и радиальные улицы. Критические места это точки пересечения, больших радиальных ули (Тверская, Мясницкая, и т. д.) с окружностью (бул варами). Здесь выросли площади, которые требую утилизации без торможения движения, особенно сгу щенного в этих местах (см. план). Здесь место цент ральных учреждений. Здесь родилась идея предлага емого типа.

Конструкция

Для устойчивого положения свободно баланси рующего тела, необходимы и достаточны 3 точк опоры*). Поэтому мы ограничились тремя стойкам с открытыми каналами лифтов и патерностеро между ними застекленный канал лестничных клето Стойки опираются системой катков и ребер на фу дамент. (Принцип упругих ферм и мостовых ко струкций). Одна стойка заключена под землей межд линиями метрополитена и служит ему станцией У других двух остановки трамвая. Структура верхне рабочей части (бюро, учреждения): скелетная цен ральная труба, открытая от пола до верхнего све внутри, несет балконы корридоров; т. е. выйдя и лифта в первом этаже можно читать №№ на двер помещений 2-го и 3-го этажей. На этой центрально раме консолями держатся горизонтальные площад этажей. Все тело, как вагон положено на стойки.

Материал

Скелет из новых сортов нержавеющей и выде живающей высокия напряжения стали (Крупп). Легки и хорошо изолирующие на тепло-и звукопроводност материалы для междуэтажных перекрытий и перег родок. Стекло химически обработанное для пропуск световых и задержки тепловых лучей.

Каче-

Все элементы скелета нормированы и поэтом по мере потребности застройки новой площади н линии кольца А или Б, остается лишь произвест

*) Одна ножка четырехногого стола висит в воздухе.

Конструкция небоскреба.

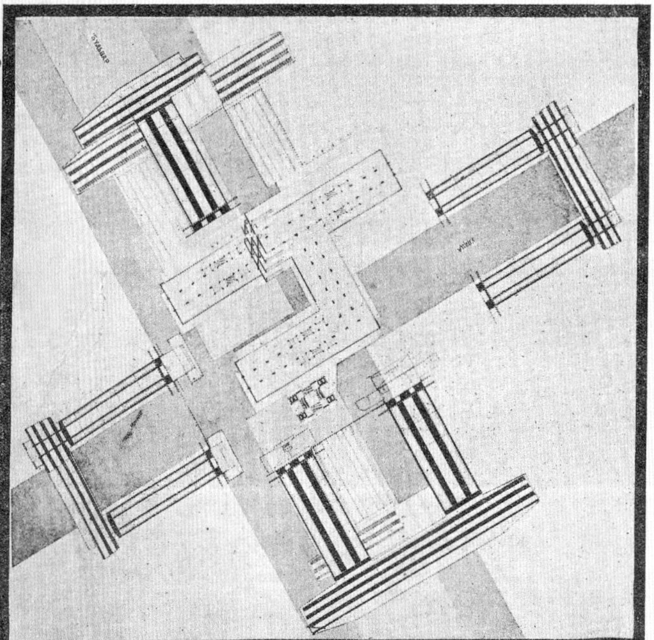

План центра Москвы с небоскребами по кольцу А.

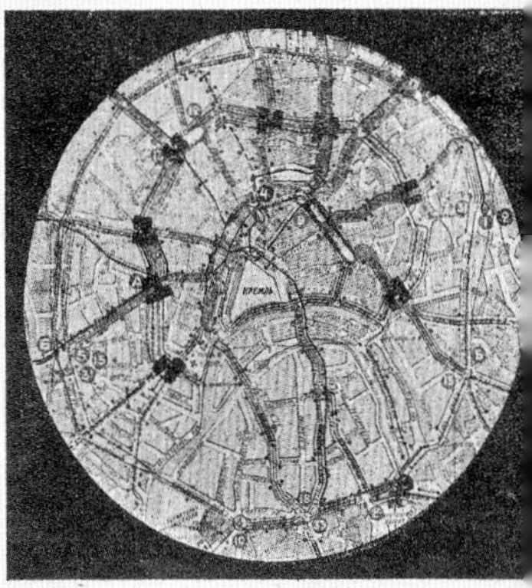

онтаж готовых частей. Монтаж может производиться ЕЗ ЛЕСОВ: до наводки верхних форм стойки держатся на тросах. Поэтому стройка может итти не перерывая движения площади. Затем по отношению существующим постройкам то качество, что их почти не нужно сносить. Огромные преимущества наличии света и воздуха по отношению к американскому башенному типу небоскреба.

1. При пластическом оформлении этого сооружения, я учитывал конструкцию лишь как один из первичных элементов в достижении необходимого полезного действия (механического эффекта). Я бы той-же логической последовательностью, так же удовлетворяя всем утилитарным требованиям мог выбрать другую конструкцию*), если-б хотел достигнуть другого эстетического эффекта.

2. Я считаю, что в своей основе сила эстетического эффекта определяется не качеством и не количеством,—это есть состояние, температура.

3. Я исходил из равновесия двух пар контрастов:

а) Город состоит из атрофирующихся старых частей и растущих живых, новых. Этот контраст мы хотим углубить.

б) Дать самому сооружению пространственное равновесие, как результат контрастных вертикальных и горизонтальных напряжений.

4. Дать новый масштаб городу, в котором человек сегодня больше не мерит собственным локтем, а сотнями метров.

5. Элементарно организовать сооружение из ребер, плоскостей и об'емов, сквозных, прозрачных и плотных, вместе составляющих однозначную пространственную систему.

Перспектива вдоль бульвара.

6. Со всех основных 6-ти точек зрения данное сооружение однозначно характеризовано:

Схема формы при виде: По направлению:

1. Сверху	2. Снизу	3. К Кремлю	4. От Кремля	5. Вдоль бульвара	6. В обратную сторону:

Такая характеристика делает ориентировку по этим сооружениям в городе совершенно ясной. При установке всей серии, введение цвета для отметки каждого небоскреба в отдельности послужит к усилению его ориентировочных качеств.

*) В выработке и расчете конструкции мне помогал ЭМИЛЬ РООТ (Цюрих), которому я рад и здесь выразить свою признательность.

В следующей серии (W B 2) будет показана совершенно другая конструкция.

Этот проэкт (Wolkenbügel) был впервые демонстрирован на выставке Ноябрьской группы в Берлине, затем на международной выставке современной архитектуры в Мангейме.

CHOBASNOWACHOBASNOWACHOBASNOWACHOBASNOWACHOBASNOWACHOBASNOWACHOBASNOWACHOBASNOWACHOBASNOWACHOBASNOWACHOBASNOWACHOBASNOWA

Основы построения теории Архитектуры

(Под знаком рационалистической эстетики)

Н. ЛАДОВСКИЙ

Архитектурная рацинальность зиждется на экономическом принципе так же, как и техническая рациональность. Разница заключается в том, что техническая рациональность есть экономия труда и материала при создании целесообразного сооружения, а архитектурная рациональность есть экономия психической энергии при восприятии пространственных и функциональных свойств сооружения. Синтез этих двух рациональностей в одном сооружении и есть рацио-архитектура.

Часть I. О ФОРМЕ.

При восприятии материальной формы как таковой мы одновременно можем усмотреть в ней выразительность качеств:

1) геометрических — отношения сторон, ребер, углов, характер поверхностей и т. д.

2) физических—весомость, плотность, массу, и т. д.

3) физико-механических—устойчивость, подвижность,

4) логических—выразительности поверхности как таковой и ограничивающей об'ем . . . .

. . . .

В зависимости от выразительности величины количества мы можем говорить о:

а) мощи и слабости,

б) величии и низменности,

в) конечности и безконечности. . .

. . . .

. . . .

2. Архитектура оперирует этими „качествами" как определенными величинами. Архитектор конструирует форму внося элементы, которые не являются техническими или утилитарными в обычном смысле слова и которые можно рассматривать как „архитектурные мотивы". В архитектурном отношении эти „мотивы" должны быть рациональны и служить высшей технической потребности человека **ориентироваться в пространстве** . . . .

Для иллюстрации одного из видов работы над геометрической выразительностью формы рассмотрим

Черт. № 1.

Пример 1.

3. Две проекции параллелопипеда дают о нем точное геометрическое **представление — образ** (черт. № 1).

Реальная перспектива его, представленная в ряде статических моментов 1. 2. . . черт. № 2, дает приближенный образ, стремящийся к геометрическому, выраженному в двух проекциях, как к своему пределу.

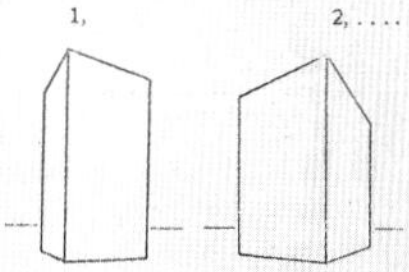

Черт. № 2.

4. Работа архитектора над геометрической выразительностью формы, которую мы всегда воспринимаем в перспективе, заключается в приближении образа получаемого от восприятия реальной перспективы к образу, данному в проекциях.

Степенность приближения зависит от количества и качества, входящих в конструируемую архитектором систему определения—элементов-признаков. Материалом этой системы элементов-признаков, обычно служит в сооружении видимая техническая конструкция. Там, где она может быть использована полностью создается синтез техники и архитектуры, где этого

ВОЛОДЬКО

ЛАВРОВ

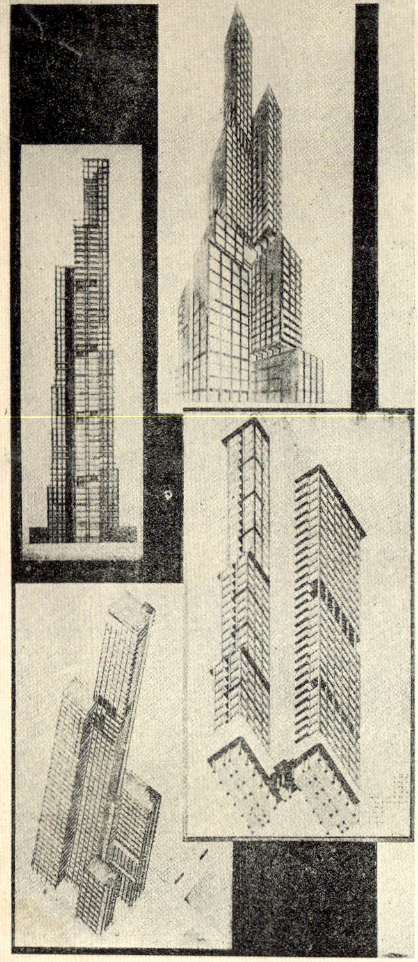

ГЛУЩЕНКО

ПОПОВ

ПРОЕКТЫ НЕБОСКРЕБОВ ДЛЯ В.С.Н.Х. У СТРЕТЕНСКИХ ВОРОТ,

мастерская Н. А. Ладовского (1924—25 Вхутемас).

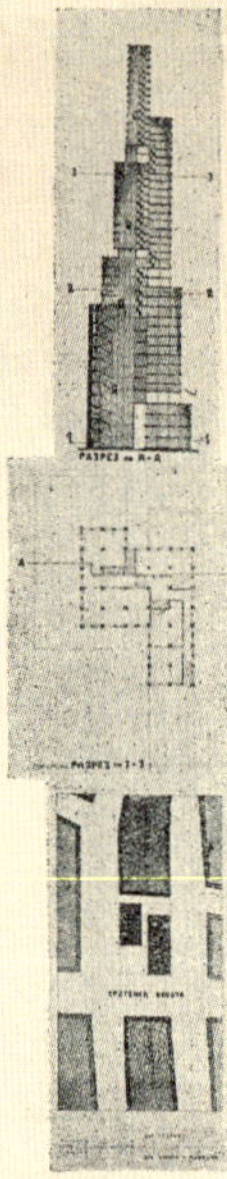

ЛАВРОВ

ВОЛОДЬКО

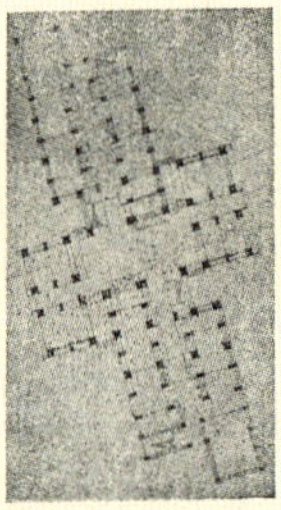

Небоскребы СССР и Америки

Небоскреб для СССР является в настоящее время проблемой, а действительностью ВСНХ строит в Харьк небоскреб для технических и торговых контор. „Извест строят небоскреб на Страстной пл. в Москве, Госбанк пр полагает об'явить конкурс на постройку небоскреба.

Пока небоскребы СССР не выше 10—16 этажей их к струкция и эксплоатация мало чем отличаются от су ствующих высоких домов. Но при постройке более высо возникает ряд сложных технических вопросов, из котор наименее разрешены вопросы пожарной безопасности и в можности быстрой разгрузки масс, в определенный мом пред н—бом, без нарушения общего движения улицы. В жарном отношении особенно уязвимым местом являю лифты, если они построены в особых шахтах, и лесничн клетки, которые служат во время пожара как дымо трубы. Имеются попытки устройства с каждой площа лестниц наружных балконов, которые во время пожара с жат спасательными островами. Более действительным ср ством противопожарной защиты могут быть: а) предлагаем мною коленчатые в вертикальном разрезе лестничные кле с автомотически закрывающимися в коленах двер (черт. № 1).

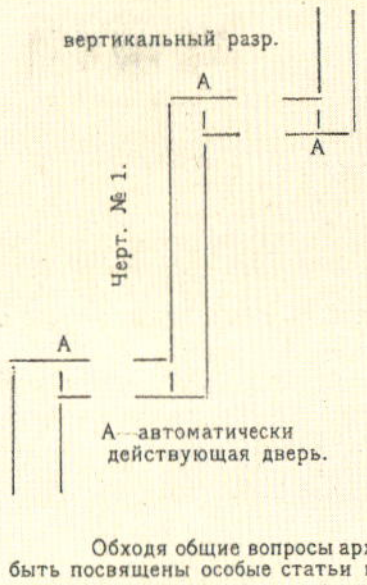

Черт. № 1.

А—автоматически действующая дверь.

б) Вынос лестнич клеток и лифтов нару соединяя их с корпу перекидными галлерея с автоматически закры ющимися дверьми.

Вопрос о разгрузке ловеческих масс мо быть разрешен, остав нием незастроенным вс или части первого эта Могущее возникнуть ражения о не рациона ности этой меры, в смы потери доходности и у личение стоимости со жения, не заслужив особого внимания, т. потеря одного этажа разится слишком неб шим процентом,ввиду б шой общей высоты со жения.

Обходя общие вопросы архитектуры, которым дол быть посвящены особые статьи необходимо здесь косну лишь некоторых сторон, являющихся специфическими архитектуры н-бов. Архитектура не должна маскиров конструкции, как это делают американцы, она должна б „правдива". Но наивно было бы думать, что достато „честно" показывать конструкцию, чтобы достичь архи ктурных целей.

Выразительность высоты является основной п лемой н-ба. Невольно возникают образы готических храм где эта проблема разрешалась. Недаром американцы любят применять готические мотивы в обработке фаса своих н-бов. Архитекторы готики материализовали в ка идею устремленности к богу, который мыслился на небе Мистицизм, которым было проникнуто средневековье, ностью отразился в архитектурных формах ея. Но ко современный банк или редакция газеты, или универ напяливают на себя архитектурные формы готики, то выглядит в современности также, как выглядел бы дирек банка в кардинальском облачении. Высота должна т ктоваться лишь как смелое движение кверху, преодоление тяжести, как достижение техни

НЕБОСКРЕБОВНЕБОСКРЕБОВНЕБОСКРЕБОВНЕБОСКРЕБОВНЕБОСКРЕБОВНЕБОСКРЕБОВНЕБОСКРЕБОВ НЕБОСКРЕБОВ НЕБОСКРЕБОВ НЕБОСКРЕБОВНЕБОСКРЕБОВНЕ

нельзя, там архитектурная конструкция (элементы-признаки) создается рельефными членениями поверхности формы, как наиболее технически простым и экономным средством исполнения. Конкретным примером постановки и решения задач такого рода могут служить задания, данные мною впервые в 1920 г. на Архфаке ВХУТЕМАС'а.

Задание № 1 (Форма архитектурно-геометрическая).

5. Дано:

1. Правильный параллелопипед в горизонтальной проэкции представляющий квадрат 20x20 м., высота 30 м.
2. Высота глаз зрителя 1,60 м., разстояние точки зрения не более 30 м., точка зрен. подвижна, скорость не более 15 м. в с.
3. Освещение солнечное.

Прим. При решении задания необходимо принять во внимание движение солнца и возможность такого его положения, при котором одновременно могут быть равномерно освещены две стороны п-да.

Требуется показать зрителю:

1. Направление поверхностей, образующих стороны п-да по отношению к координатным плоскостям (пространственную ориентацию).

   Прим.: Пространственные координаты теже, что приняты в теории перспективы.
2. Ясную читку ребер.
3. Равенство сторон.
4. Отношение стороны основания к высоте
5. Правильность поверхностей, образующих стороны.
6. Прямизну углов (т. е., что углы равны 90о).

Средствами выражения могут быть: вертикальные и горизонтальные членения, светотень и фактура поверхностей.

Требуется представить:

1. Модель или перспективный вид.
2. Чертежи 2-х фасадов, образующих взаимно угол.
3. Разр. гор. и верт. Масштаб 1:100.

20. X—1920 г. Н. Л.

6. Как видно из задания, основной работой в нем является выявление для зрителя геометрических качеств п—да. Но что означает **выявить геометрический образ?** Разве в математически правильно построенном п—де мы увидим какую либо иную форму—шар, конус, цилиндр и т. п. Нет, мы в нем не увидим ни шара, ни цилиндра и т. д., но мы также не увидим п—да с теми геометрическими качествами, которые даны в задании. Достаточно взглянуть на перспективный ряд 1, 2, . . . (черт. № 2), чтобы убедиться в недостаточности признаков, по которым можно было бы определить: что стороны основания равны, что отношение высоты к стороне основания = 1,5:1.

Можно ли допустить, чтобы архитектор строя форму не знал как ее будет воспринимать зритель? Такое допущение означало бы полную безпринципность и невозможность какого бы то ни было мастерства в области геометрической выразительности. Необходимо установить положение, что **архитектурно-геометрическая сторона материальной формы заключается в такой ея проработке, при которой зритель действительно видит ее геометрическую характеристику в той мере, в которой это необходимо для данного случая.**

Что для этого нужно сделать в данном приме

7. Необходимо поставить знак тождества ме каждой парой одновременно видимых сто п—да, следовательно между всеми сторонами его.

Это означает, что членения на поверхности в сторон п—да должны быть тождественны . . . .

Если, для примера, мы впишем по окружнос на каждую из сторон п—да, так, (черт. № 3). чтобы зритель мог при восприятии определить раве ство диаметров каждой пары одновременно вид окружностей, то этим будет дана некая **степе приближения образа к его геометрической сущнос** будет более уяснено равенство расстояний отдельн ребер от переднего ребра . . . .

Вписав еще по пол'окружности черт. № 4:

Черт. 4. Черт. 3.

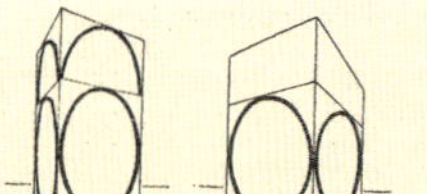

мы уясним от шение основан к высоте 1: равенство стор и все выте ющие следств **все в извести степени прибл жения**, какое м гут дать эти э менты . . . (

. . . .

Продолжая таким образом анализ далее мы н дем и остальные элементы, необходимые для решен задания . . . .

Лубянка, Стретенка, Мясницкая, являются большими жизненными артериями города, они нуждаются в большом количестве концентрированных торговых и конторских помещений. Наглядно это иллюстрируется стихийно нелепой стройкой на углу Лубянской площади и Мясницкой ул.

Несомненно, самым правильным решением вопроса обслуживания центральной части города, будет постройка небоскреба на Лубянской пл. Благодаря высокому положению площади н-б будет виден со многих сторон, что обезпечивает его главное качество: ориентировочность. Для безхарактерной в настоящем виде площади, небоскреб даст тон остальным строениям и повлияет на форму площади, которая должна стремиться к неравностороннему треугольнику, в одной из вершин которого и будет стоять небоскреб. **На Лубянской пл. угол Мясницкой, на уч. № 1 необходимо построить небоскреб В.С.Н.Х.**

Небоскреб на Лубянской площади

Проект

В. Ф. КРИНСКОГО.

1923

Масштабность является одним из средств выразительности величины. Американцы разрешают вопрос о масштабности тем, что используют „стандартизованные" элементы, каковыми являются окна, как меру величины. В таком разрешении вопроса о масштабности кроется основная причина, заставляющая их маскировать конструкцию и затрудняющая разрешение целого ряда других планировочных вопросов, в конце концов, не разрешая и основного вопроса о масштабности, т. к. в „стандартизованном" элементе окна нет признаков функционально связывающих его с ростом человека.

Если отбросить все нелепое, что пристало по недоразумению к поверхности н-ба, то останется основной конструктивный скелет, определяемый действием сил тяжести и витраж. Эти элементы, по принципу экономии, должны являться элементами и архитектуры. При настоящем положении архитектуры вообще мы не можем пред'являть к ней особых требований и в н-бе. Элементарное же требование, которое мы должны пред'явить к архитектурной обработке поверхности, состоящей из стоек, балок и витража, есть положение, что конструктивные элементы, составляющие фасад н-ба должны быть подчинены пространственной логике. Помимо непосредственной технической функции этих элементов, они должны содержать и архитектурную функцию — выражать пространственное соотношение с надлежащей степенью точности. Пренебрежение этим положением в обработке поверхности лишает ее основных архитектурных качеств. Отрицательным примером подхода к решению поверхности может служить обработка представленная рис. № 6 А.

Поверхность не имеет глубины, дан один только план.

Не следует понимать, что такое решение вообще недопустимо в архитектуре. Отрицательность этого примера надо понимать в том смысле, что такого рода прием не может быть основным, но может быть употребляем как подсобный: фон разрыв, вставка и т. п.

Если мы примем это первое положение, то из него следует, что архитектурная обработка поверхности должна быть рельефна. Всякое рельефное расчленение поверхности вызывает необходимость пространственной организации ея, для облегчения и направления внимания воспринимающего эту поверхность. Два принципа имеют большое значение в пространственной организации поверхности, принцип перспективный и принцип наложения. Элементарным примером решения поверхности по первому принципу может служить прием черт. № 3.

НЕБОСКРЕБОВНЕБОСКРЕБОВНЕБОСКРЕБОВНЕБОСКРЕБОВНЕБОСКРЕБОВНЕБОСКРЕБОВНЕБОСКРЕБОВНЕБОСКРЕБ

Работа студ. Петрова, руководство Н. Л. (Вхутемас 1920 г.).

Сравнивая архитектурные образы, полученные в результате такой обработки с перспективным рядом 1, 2, . . . (черт. № 2), при тех же условиях зрения, можно убедиться в большей степени приближения образа архитектурного (черт. № 4) к образу, данному в проекциях, черт. 1. . . . .

. . . .

Действие света на моделировку общепонятна. В данном задании поставлено определенное требование § 3. Решение возможно:

а) или различной фактурной обработкой каждой пары одновременно видимых поверхностей . . . (4)

б) или расчленением одной из каждых двух одновременно видимых поверхностей на участки, составляющие угол к поверхности, часть которой они составляют . . . . (5)

в) или расчленением обеих одновременно видимых поверхностей, как в п. (5), но углы частных поверхностей одной стороны не равны углам ч. п. другой . . . . (6)

Пример решения

8. В приведенном решении Петрова §§ 1, 2, 3, 6 задания выявлены следующими средствами:

§ 1 и 2 двукратным повторением горизонтальных проекций п-да.

§ 5 прямолинейными вертикальными и горизонтальными, взаимно перпендикулярными, членениями поверхностей.

§ 6 показанием в углах горизонтальных проекций, видимых снизу небольших квадратов, которые оцениваются как таковые непосредственно в силу малой величины их, для усиления в них вписаны малые окружности.

Дела Асновы

Устав Ассоциации Новых Архитекторов „АСНОВА" утвержден Отделом Управления Моссовета Р. К. и К. Д. и зарегистрирован 1923 г. июля 23 дня за № 2098/4.

За указаннне время общих собраний было 23.

Отдельных наиболее важных решений принято:

1. Участие членов Аснова в разработке проэктов Международного Красного Стадиона на Ленинских горах в Москве.
2. Участие на Международной Выставке Декоративных Искусств в Париже в 1925 г. (За экспонаты Аснова удостоена золотой медали).
3. Разработка вопроса об увековечении памяти Ленина в архитектуре.
4. Работа членов Аснова в построении нового метода и программы Вхутемаса.
5. Организация архитектурного отделения в ГИК'е.
6. Постановка вопроса об реорганизации архитектурных конкурсов в связи с Кодексом Труда СССР.
7. Разработка положения об авторском праве: предложено МАО, ЛАО и ВАИ организовать совместную комиссию.
8. Поднят вопрос пред Моссоветом об урегулировании фасадов и улиц в связи с ремонтом и новым строительством.
9. Обмен мнениями межлу Асновой и рядом крупных новаторов современной архитектуры заграницей по вопросу о желательности созывв в СССР международной конференции по вопросам архитектуры.
10. Вступление в Аснову ряда архитекторов Германии, Голландии, Франции.
11. Издание газеты „Аснова".
12. Взять на себя организацию архитектурсекции на выставке „Общества 4-х искусств".

Состоялись следующие доклады и собеседования:

1. Арх. Нагорский: „Значение сырцово-глиняных построек в разрешении жилищного кризиса".
2. Арх. Рухлядев: „Реорганизация архитектурных конкурсов".
3. Худ. Штернберг: „Западное искусство" впечатления о заграничной поездке".
4. Арх. Ладовский: „Рационализм и конструктивизм в архитектуре".
5. Арх-ра Рухлядев и Балихин: „Увековечение памяти Ленина в архитектуре".
6. Инж. Кузьмин: „Постройка сборочных мастерских аэропланного завода".
7. Группа студентов: „Летняя практика на постройке аэропланного завода".
8. Группа студентов: „Постройка Всероссийской Сельско-Хозяйственной Выставки".
9. Группа членов Аснова преподавателей Вхутемаса: „Программа и методы образования на пространственном концентре основного отделения Вхутемаса".
10. Собеседование об отчетной выставке 2-го отделения Архфака Вхутемаса".
11. Арх. Лисицкий: „Современная архитектура Европы и Америки". Впечатления заграничной поездки.
12. Арх. Мельников: „Постройка Советского павильона на Междун. Выставке Декор. Искус. в Париже".
13. Арх. Шибаев: „Постройка рынка на Цветном бульваре".

Аснова организовала следующие секции:

1. Идеологическая секция. В данный период обсуждаются тезисы по вопросу „Инженерия и архитектура" (т.т. Балихин, Ламцов, Рухлядев).

   На очереди вопросы: О выразительности архитектурной формы. Цели, задачи и содержание работ Асновы. Методы архитектурного образования.
2. Секция транспортной архитектуры. Производит работу над архитектурным оформлением дирижабля Циалковского (Лисицкий и Крутиков в контакте с инженером Виноградовым).

   Организуются секции: по жилищному строительству, по градостроительству.

По предложению т. Ладовского, Аснова считает полезным организацию психо-технической лаборатории для исследования архитектурных форм и их воздействия; т. Ладовскому поручено осуществление этой работы.

Такая обработка поверхности дает первую степень выразительности глубины: горизонтальные членения шире вертикальных и, следовательно, читаются, как стоящие на первом плане по отношению к вертикальным.

Черт. № 3.

Примером второго подхода к решению может служить черт. № 4 сдесь дана более высокая степень выразительности глубины: узкие вертикальные членения, показаны на первом плане, широкие горизонтальные на втором (принцип наложения).

Черт. № 4.

Чертеж № 5 дает решение на основе совмещения обоих принципов.

Черт. № 5.

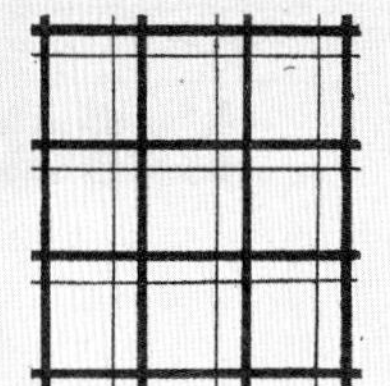

Мастера старого времени разрешали подобные задачи системой ордеров или другими, более или менее декоративными, элементами. Убедительным примером решения подобной задачи можно считать Палаццо Вальмарано архитект. Палладио. (По принципу наложения и перспективы организован фасад системою трех ордеров).

В работах современных американских архитекторов тщетно было бы искать какой нибудь принципиальности в этой области. Единственно что ими руководит, это убеждение в спасительности „мотивов" ренесанса и готики, употребляемых ими в условиях совершенно несходных с теми, каковые были у мастеров их создавших.

Германия является второй страной признавшей н-бы жизненным явлением. Хотя ея строительная деятельность в этом отношении незначительна, однако она успела внести некоторые технико-планировочные коррективы в это дело. В архитектурном отношении Германию нельзя упрекнуть в безидейности, наоборот, ее можно упрекнуть в обратном, в слишком большом увлечении идеологизмами, что мешает подняться мастерству. Германец видит поверхность слишком сложно психологически, чтобы различать ее как пространственную величину.

Вопрос об основных контрастах в н-бе легче всего разрешается в сопоставлении об'емности и пространственности. Здесь полезно сделать некоторые сравнения из истории архитектуры. Мотив рустованной колонны, выразительность ея об'ема, массы и мощи были найдены случайно, когда пришлось оставить в незаконченном виде колонны какого-то римского храма. Впоследствии в ранесансе часто пользовались сознательно этим мотивом рустованной колонны, для придания определенной выразительности. Американцы моглибы сделать подобное открытие если бы они взглянули на строющийся ими н-б (рис. № 6).

Контраст между необлицованной частью и заполненной облицовкой так велик, архитектурная выразительность степеней тяжелого так сильна, что решение само собой напрашивается.

На этом пункте стройки, казалось, следовало бы остановится и завершить лишь техническую и утилитарную сторону сооружения.

Рис. № 6.

Несмотря на кажущуюся техническую смелость постройки н-бов Нью-Иорка, в общем, технико-конструктивная сторона их стоит далеко не на той высоте, на которой это было бы возможно при современном состоянии строительной техники вообще. Об этом свидетельствуют нам жалобы молодых архитекторов, пробуждающихся к новому в самой Америке. Как видно, наиболее талантливые конструкторы не находят для себя интересным работать над конструкцией, которая сплошь замаскирована и уходят в мосто,-аэро и автостроительство.

Надо надеяться, что СССР в технике строительства н-бов пойдет по более смелым путям, а в архитектуре их неизбежно по пути **рационализма**.

2/IV—26 г. Энаэль.

Задание № 2 (Форма архитектурно-геометрическая).

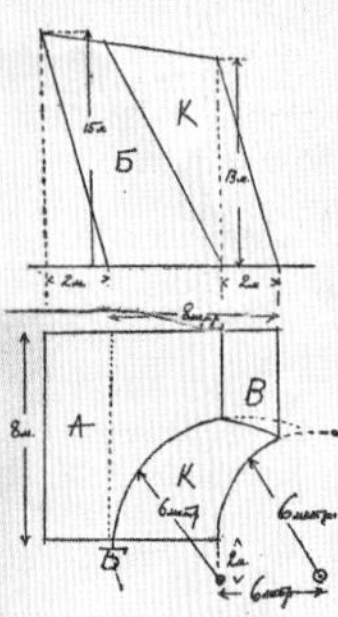

Черт. № 4.

9. Дано:

1. Прилагаемый чертеж геометрической формы.
2. Горизонт зрения нормальный, точка зрения подвижна, ск. не более 15 м. макс. разстояние т. з. 30 м.
3. Освещение солнечное.

Требуется показать зрителю:

1. Все плоскости, как таковые.
2. Плокости А и Б как образующие угол.
3. Наклонность плоскости В.
4. Цилиндричность или конусовидность поверхности К.
5. Ясную читку всех углов.

Необходимо представить:

Макет и чертежи в м. 1:100.

Вхутемас.
30/X—1920 г.

Н. Л.

Дома или улицы?

Открытое письмо Моссовету.

Со времени Октябрьской революции прошло 8 лет, за это время Россия превратилась в СССР, однако облик городов СССР ничем не отличается от таковых России.

Как только революция стала выходить из острого экономического кризиса, стала усиливаться строительная деятельность. Эта деятельность, правда, относилась, главным образом, к восстановлению разрушающихся зданий, к ремонту и лишь в незначительной степени к строительству нового.

В этой незначительной деятельности имеется одна сторона, приобретающая значение архитектурное и социальное. Не надо обладать никакими специальными знаниями, не нужно собирать никакого статистического материала, чтобы убедиться в том, что хотя бы в одной Москве затрачивались большие средства на окраску фасадов зданий. Можно утверждать, что в течении последних 4-х лет 15% всех фасадов г. Москвы были перекрашены наново.

Но во всей этой деятельности, имеющей главным образом архитектурное значение, не было никакого плана, никакой идеи, никакого руководства. Предоставленные самим себе жилтоварищества рассматривали свои владения, как самостоятельное целое, ничего общее неимющее ни со своими соседями, ни с улицей, как таковой. Такой взгляд переносится и на новое строительство, Новые сооружения рассматриваются также, как обособленные комплексы неосуществляющие идеи новой улицы как целостной системы.

АСНОВА учитывает, что осуществление перепланировки городов требует больших затрат и потому невыполнимо в ближайшее время, но частично идея изменения индивидуалистического характера домов, соответственно строю жизни единственной в мире Советской республики уже может проводиться в жизнь, не вызывая никаких специальных расходов и риска навязывания какой-либо недостаточно обоснованной идеи.

АСНОВА считает необходимым обратить внимание Моссовета на **окраску зданий.**

Необходимо ввести определенно разработанный план в систему окраски улиц. Основным принципом этого плана должно быть об'единение фасадов, составляющих целостную систему, определяющую улицу, а не выделение отдельных ничего общего между собою неимеющих владений. Каждая улица может иметь свой основной тон, в котором могут быть модуляции и нарушения (разрывы), в зависимости от особенностей отдельных сооружений. Сооружения облицованные дорогими материалами или имитирующими их, а также имеющие археологическое значение и находящиеся под охраной комиссии по сохранению памятников старины, могут остаться неприкосновенными.

Некоторые сооружения имеющие особое значение, как например вокзалы, госучреждения и т. п. д. могут быть наоборот выделены особой окраской в зависимости от окружающей обстановки и архитектуры их.

Разработанный план окраски зданий вносится на утверждение и проводится в жизнь теми же организациями, которые ведают коммунальным строительством.

Осуществляется план в жизни постепенно по мере производства окраски фасадов отдельными жилтовариществами. Таким образом можно расчитывать, что Москва может изменить свой облик через ближайшие несколько лет, приблизив его к тому, который отличает социалистическое строительство от анархо-капиталистического.

В защиту конкурентов

Возрождающееся архитектурное строительство Республики и стремление к привлечению всех творческих сил к открытому соревнованию, вызывает наблюдаемое обилие архитектурных конкурсов и общий интерес к ним.

В дореволюционное время как у нас, так и на Западе продукт получаемый в результате конкурсов мало удовлетворял как заказчиков, так и конкурентов. Так называемая „свобода творчества", которая казалось при конкурсе должна была быть наиболее обеспечена, на самом деле была фикцией, так как одна часть задания захватывалась самой программой, а другая—определялась воспитанием судей. Так называемая „свобода труда" (каждому желающему предоставлялось право участия в конкурсе) также была фикцией, так как возможность участия в работе зависела от материальной обеспеченности архитектора, бравшегося за дело без гарантии оплаты.

Составление программы, установление количества и величины премий, само жюрирование,—все это имело существенные недостатки также неблагоприятно отражавшиеся на результате. „Об'ективность" жюри было того же порядка, как и вышеназванные „свободы".

Положение трудящегося в СССР перестраивается с основания. Это требует пересмотра и вопросов „свободы труда" и „свободы творчества", которые в практике конкурсного дела до сих пор остаются не измененными. Конституция конкурсного дела в целом осталась и по сей день незыблемой, но все противоречия этой системы обострились до крайности.

НАШИ ПРЕДЛОЖЕНИЯ.

К ПРОГРАММЕ.

Для обеспечения „свободы творчества", которую мы понимаем как творческую инициативу, необходимо найти форму участия самих конкурентов в разработке программы задания. Организаторы конкурса об'являют тему, участок и требуемую кубатуру. Дальнейшая разработка и уточнение производится путем вопросов конкурентов и ответов организаторов. И все-же программа никогда не с'умеет охватить всех возможных решений: она всегда должна оставлять место чрезвычайному предложению.

К ПРЕМИЯМ.

Для обеспечения „свободы труда", которую следует понимать, как одинаковую экономическую возможность для всех желающих принимать участие в конкурсе, необходимо найти рациональное распределение ассигнованной на конкурс суммы. Материальная сторона соревнования должна быть сконцентрирована на одной значительной премии (для постройки нужен один проект), которая выдается за относительно лучший проект соответствующий программе конкурса. Другая премия должна выдаваться за проект не следующий буквально программе, но заключающий в себе чрезвычайное предложение. Остальная сумма составляет по возможности значительное количество небольших равных премий гарантирующих минимальную оплату труда и материала. Такая система может лишь положительно действовать и на качество продукта.

К ЖЮРИ.

Роль жюри должна сводится лишь к организации конкурса и его проведению. Роль экспертизы переходит в другие руки. Оценка поступившего на конкурс материала по существу является судопроизводством. Гражданское и уголовное судопроизводство в настоящее время является наиболее совершенной формой этой процедуры. Поэтому всякое совершенствование системы жюрирования должно базироваться на использовании судопроизводственных форм. Это касается как состава, так и ведения жюрирования.

Как в обычном судопроизводстве имеются стороны, судьи, прокурор, защитник и заседатели, так аналогично в архитектурном конкурсе сторонами являются конкуренты, защитниками и обвинителями должны быть эксперты-специалисты, при чем одна группа экспертов дает положительные (защитники), другая отрицательные отзывы (прокурор), судья это председатель избранный организационным коллективом. Решающая инстанция это заседатели, являющиеся представителями всех организаций и учреждений заинтересованных в наилучшем разрешении данного вопроса.

Жюрирование.

Основное положение—публичность жюрирования, как гарантия об'ективности.

Конкуренту должно быть представлено последнее слово. Он может прислать свое суждение о заключении экспертов до окончательного присуждения премий.

Последнее положение гарантирует жюри от возможных ошибок из-за непонимания соображений руководивших автором проекта.

Присуждение премий производится не той группой, лиц, которая организовала конкурс, руководила жюрирванием и т. д., а нейтральной группой заседателей.

Психо-техническая лаборатория архитектуры

(В порядке постановки вопроса).

Архитектор должен быть, хотя бы элементарно, знаком с законами восприятия и средствами воз'действия, чтобы в своем мастерстве использовать все, что может дать современная наука. Среди наук способствующих развитию архитектуры серьезное место должна занять молодая еще наука психотехника. Этой подсобной науке, несомненно, предстоит большое поле деятельности. Во многих областях техники она завоевала себе признание. Ее влияние становится с каждым днем все более заметным благодаря тому, что она перекидывает мосты между, так называемой, чистой наукой и практической техникой.

Среди людей дела первыми прибегли к ея помощи представители крупных индустриальных и торговых предприятий Америки при отборе служащих, далее коммерсанты в области рекламы, затем педагоги при приеме и определении способностей учащихся. В настоящее время нет такой области человеческой деятельности, на которую не притязала бы психотехника.

В области эстетики работает из года в год в своей Гарвадской лаборатории известный психолог Мюнстерберг. Там проведены следующие, имеющие отношение к архитектуре, работы: Равновесие простых форм (Pierce); неравное деление (Angier); симметрия (Puffer); повторение пространственных форм (Rowland); вертикальное деление (Dawis); простые ритмические формы и т. д.

Работы произведенные мною, а затем и моими товарищами, во ВХУТЕМАС'е с 1920 г. в области архитектуры, проверенные методами психотехники помогут научной постановке положений архитектуры, на основе рационалистической эстетики.

Самым правильным подходом к решению этого вопроса будет организация психо-технической лаборатории для изучения вопросов рациональной архитектуры при „**Аснова**". В подтверждение своевременности постановки этого вопроса считаю наилучшим привести слова Мюнстерберга: „Психотехника не может создавать художников....., но она всем им может дать опорный пункт для того, чтобы самым верным образом достичь известных целей, к которым они стремятся и вернее всего избежать известных опасностей...... Широко развитая психотехника может в будущем ставить свои требования композиторам, хотя бы постоянно подтверждалось, что гений находит бессознательно то, что наука вырабатывает с большим трудом".

Помимо чисто научного значения какое может иметь работа лаборатории, ея деятельность должна иметь и практическое значение в архитектурной повседневности.

Сколько недоразумений лаборатория могла бы устранить при оценке качеств архитектурной работы из за отсутствия общеобязательной терминологии даже в среде специалистов. Случайность оценки конкурсных проектов общеизвестна. Страсти возникающие между педагогами и учащимися на почве взаимного непонимания, не могут быть устранены до правильной постановки работы лаборатории. Психотехническая лаборатория во всех этих и многих других случаях может сыграть большую подсобную роль.

Москва, 29/III—26 г. **Н. Ладовский**

Викинг Эггелинг

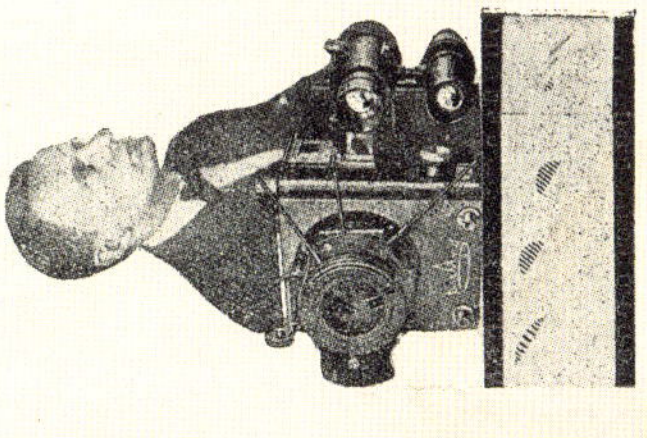

Аснова в своем научном концентре обнимает все работы над элементами пластического оформления и ветствует все изобретения в этой области. Работа покойного Эггелинга особо ценна нам: он изучал законы пространственного членения и движения, т. е основы тектоники. Он это реализовал новым оптическим инструментом—кино. Этим он открыл путь целому ряду новых возможностей так же и в области архитектурного воспитания. Безусловно, что работа Эггелинга является самым значительным изобретением западного искусства после кубистического периода.

19 мая в Берлине умер Викинг Эггелинг.

Впервые я услышал его имя однажды ночью 1920 года в одной из комнат Люкса (общежит. ИККИ), от молодого немецкого товарища только что проскочившего к нам через все блокады. Это были первые вести с Запада после 6 лет изоляции. Расказывая мне об Эйнштейне и Шпенглере, он назвал Эггелинга, с которым встретился в Мюнхене в короткие дни Баварской Советской Республики. Эггелинг изобрел и работал над „абсолютным" фильмом. Он хотел обратиться за помощью для осуществления своей работы в Россию.

Вначале 1922 г. мы встретились в Берлине. Небольшой, сухой, с отлично чеканенным интернациональным черепом—он не был похож на шведа. О своей работе он говорил очень мало. Я предложил ему и его сотруднику Гансу Рихтеру сотрудничать в журнале „ВЕЩЬ" (см. № 2—3, 1922 г. Берлин). Эггелинг уже давно работал над анализом законов плоскостной композиции и динамики. Стремление к пластичеткому оформлению движения (проблема поставленная уже итальянскими футуристами) нашла в нем простое и прекрасное разрешение. Он переменил и инструмент и метод. Вместо этюдника с тюбами красок—киноаппарат, вместо обрамленного грунтованного холста—экран и сколько угодно лент, которые бегут в один и тот же час во всех частях света.

В Эггелинге текла кровь музыкантов и это сказалось в его фильме. Несколько элементарных форм, нот (он думал о возможности создания пластической азбуки, из которой можно было-б образовать слоги, слова и фразы), которые как фуга рождаются, нарастают, варииируют в определенном и меняющемся темпе и ритме. Все это действие развивается в плоскости экрана и пробегает мимо нас параллельно плоскости зрения. Таким образом фильм Эггелинга геометрически двухмерен + время. Ему пришлось проделать страшно кропотливую работу чтобы реализовать первые 100 метров. Нужно было сделать тысячи и тысячи рисунков и без конца корректировать с'емки.

Мы собирались вместе взяться за одну работу. Я указывал на необходимость введения третьей координаты—глубины. На отношение к свету проэктирующего аппарата не только как к средству, но как к материалу. Последнее сообщение от Эггелинга я получил из Берлина, что он собирается работать над цветным фильмом и что ему демонстрировали прекрасный аппарат для этого. В тоже время его „диагональный" фильм с большим успехом демонстрировали в ряде городов.

19-го мая приехав в Берлин, я застал Эггелинга умирающим.

На Западе целый ряд художников работает дальше в области изобретения Эггелинга. В истории развития пластических искусств место Викинга Эггелинга можно точно очертить: это переход от двухмерной станковой картины, с иллюзией третьего измерения к трехмерной иллюзорной картине экрана с реальным четвертым измерением (время).

Лисицкий

Ноябрьская группа в Берлине с большим успехом повторно устраивала 3-го и 7-го мая 25-го года вечера, на которых демонстрировались работы: Эггелинга (диагональный фильм), Ганса Рихтера, Рутмана, Гиршфельд-Мак, Леже и Морфи (Images Mobiles) и Пикабия (Entr'acte). От всех этих авторов АСНОВА имеет разрешение и обещание предоставить свои фильмы для демонстрации в СССР.

ЧЕЛОВЕК МЕРА ВСЕХ ПОРТНЫХ

ПРОБАБУШКИ ВЕРИЛИ, ЧТО ЗЕМЛЯ ЦЕНТР МИРА,
А ЧЕЛОВЕК МЕРА ВСЕХ ВЕЩЕЙ

ПРО ТАКИЕ ВЕЩИ ГОВОРИЛИ
„КАКОЙ МОГУЧИЙ ВЕЛИКАН!"

А ТАКОЕ И СЕЙЧАС СРАВНИВАЮТ НЕ ИНАЧЕ, КАК С ИСКОПАЕМЫМ ЖИВОТНЫМ.

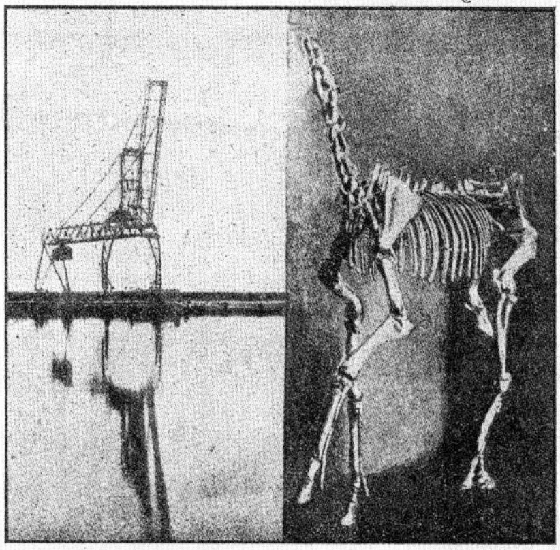

НЕ СРАВНИВАЙТЕ ЭТО НИ С КОСТЯМИ, НИ С МЯСОМ.

НАУЧИТЕСЬ ВИДЕТЬ ТО, ЧТО ПЕРЕД ВАШИМИ ГЛАЗАМИ,—

Способ употребления:
Запрокиньте голову, поднимите лист и смотрите снизу вверх, тогда увидите.

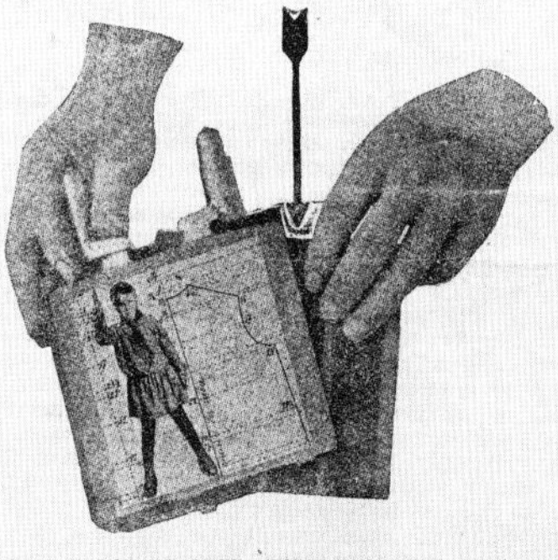

ВОТ ЧЕЛОВЕК—ПОРТНОМУ МЕРА,

а АРХИТЕКТУРУ МЕРЬТЕ АРХИТЕКТУРОЙ

ЭЛЬ.

Под редакцией: Эль Лисицкого и Н. А. Ладовского.

Мосгублит № 23990. Типография „ВХУТЕМАС", Рождественка, 11. Типооформление ЭЛЬ. Тираж 1.500 экз.

Nikolai Ladovsky
Foundations for the Construction of an Architectural Theory
(under the banner of Rationalist aesthetics)

Architectural rationality is based on the economic principle just as technical rationality is. The difference lies in the fact that technical rationality is the saving of labor and materials in the creation of a purposeful structure, whereas architectural rationality is the saving of psychic energy in the perception of the spatial and functional properties of the structure. The synthesis of these two rationalities in a single structure is what constitutes ratio-architecture.

Part I. On Form

1.
When perceiving material form as such, we can simultaneously discern in it the expressivity of qualities:
1) geometrical – the relationships of sides, edges, angles, the character of surfaces, etc.;
2) physical – weightiness, density, mass, etc.;
3) physico-mechanical – stability, mobility;
4) logical – the expressivity of the surface as such and its role in bounding volume.

Depending on their expressivity, magnitude and quantity, we can speak of:
a) power and weakness
b) grandeur and baseness
c) finitude and infinity

2.
Architecture operates with these "qualities" as specific magnitudes. The architect constructs form by introducing elements that are neither technical nor utilitarian in the usual sense, but may be considered architectural motifs. In architectural terms, these motifs must be rational and serve a higher technical necessity – the human need to orient oneself in space.

3.
For an illustration of one method of working on the geometrical expressivity of form, let us examine:

Example 1. Two projections of a parallelepiped yield an accurate geometrical representation-image of it (fig. 1).

Its real perspective, presented through a sequence of static moments 1, 2, ... (fig. 2), gives an approximated image, striving toward the geometrical one expressed in the two projections as its limit.

4.
The architect's task in enhancing the geometrical expressivity of form, which we always perceive in perspective, is to approximate the perceptual image derived from real perspective to the image conveyed in projections.

The degree of approximation depends on the quantity and quality of the element-signs entering into the system of definitions introduced by the architect. Typically, the visible technical construction of a structure serves as the material for these element-signs. Where it can be utilized fully, a synthesis of architecture and technology results; and where it cannot be fully used, architectural construction of the element-signs is created by relief components of the surface of the form, which are the technically simplest and most economical means of execution. A concrete example of setting and solving such a task is the assignment I first introduced in 1920 at the Architecture Faculty of VKhUTEMAS.

5.
Assignment No. 1
(Architectural-Geometrical Form)

Given:
1. A regular parallelepiped with a square plan of 20 × 20 m and a height of 30 m.
2. Viewer's eye level at 1.60 m, with a movable viewpoint, speed not exceeding 15 m/s, maximum viewing distance: 30 m.
3. Sunlight illumination.

Note: The solution must account for the motion of the sun and the possibility of such a position where two sides of the parallelepiped can be evenly illuminated.

Required to show the viewer:
1. The orientation of the surfaces (i.e., direction relative to coordinate planes – spatial orientation).

   Note: Spatial coordinates are the same as in the theory of perspective.

2. Clear readability of the edges.
3. Equality of the sides.
4. The ratio of the base side to the height.
5. The flatness of the surfaces forming the sides.
6. The orthogonality of the angles (i.e., all are 90°).

Means of expression may include: vertical and horizontal articulations, light and shadow, surface texture.

To be submitted:
1. Model or perspective view.
2. Drawings of the two facades forming a corner.
3. Horizontal and vertical sections.

Scale 1:100.
Dated 20/X – 1920, N. L.

6.
As is clear from the assignment, the main task is to reveal to the viewer the geometrical qualities of the parallelepiped. But what does it mean to reveal a geometrical image?

In a mathematically precise parallelepiped, would we see a sphere, cone, cylinder, etc.? Of course not. But we also would not see a parallelepiped with the particular geometrical characteristics listed in the assignment.

One need only glance at the perspective sequence 1, 2, … (fig. 2) to be convinced that the perceptual cues are insufficient to determine that the base sides are equal or that the height-to-base ratio is 1.5:1.

Can we assume that an architect constructs a form without knowing how the viewer will perceive it? Such an assumption would imply a total lack of principle, and the impossibility of mastery in the domain of geometrical expressivity.

Therefore, we must affirm: The architectural-geometrical dimension of material form lies in developing it such that the viewer truly perceives its geometric characteristics – to the degree required for the specific case.

7.
One must establish a sign of visual identity between each pair of simultaneously visible sides, and thus, between all sides of the parallelepiped.

This means that the surface subdivisions on all sides of the parallelepiped must be identical. (1)

If we inscribe circles on each face (fig. 3) such that the viewer can perceive the equality of diameters in each pair of simultaneously visible circles, then this introduces a certain degree of approximation to the geometric essence of the form. This also clarifies the equal distances from each edge to the frontal edge. (2)

By further inscribing semicircles (fig. 4), we clarify the 1:1.5 ratio between base and height, the equality of the sides, and all the logical consequences – within a known degree of approximation that these elements can achieve. (3)

By continuing the analysis, we discover the remaining elements needed to solve the assignment…

By comparing the architectural images obtained through this process with the perspective sequence (fig. 2), under identical viewing conditions, one can verify the greater proximity of the architectural image (fig. 4) to the image given by the projections (fig. 1).

The effect of light on modeling is widely understood.

In this assignment, a specific requirement is set in § 3. It may be solved:
a) either by using different surface textures on each pair of simultaneously visible sides; (4)
b) or by subdividing one of each visible pair of surfaces into segments, each at an angle to the main surface they comprise; (5)

c) either by subdividing both visible surfaces as in (5), but ensuring the angles differ on each side. (6)

8.
In the presented solution by student Petrov, sections §§ 1, 2, 5, and 6 of the assignment are clarified using the following means:

§§ 1 and 2 – through twofold repetition of the horizontal projections of the parallelepiped;

§ 5 – by means of rectilinear vertical and horizontal articulations which are mutually perpendicular;

§ 6 – by showing small squares in the corners of the horizontal projections as seen from below; these are perceived directly as squares due to their small size, and to reinforce this perception, small circles are inscribed within them.

9.
Assignment No. 2
(Architectural-Geometrical Form)

Given:
1. The attached drawing of a geometric form [fig. 6].
2. The horizon line is normal, with a mobile viewpoint, moving at a speed no more than 15 m/s, with a maximum viewing distance of 30 m.
3. Sunlight illumination.

Required to show the viewer:
1. All planes as such.
2. Planes A and B as forming an angle.
3. The inclination of plane C.
4. The cylindrical or conical nature of surface K.
5. Clear legibility of all angles.

To be submitted:
Model and drawings
Scale 1:100

Dated: VKhUTEMAS, 30/X – 1920
N. Ladovsky

Translated excerpt. Text in two parts, dated October 20 and 30, 1920. Originally published in ASNOVA Bulletin, Moscow, 1926, 3–6.

Western Eyes on Soviet Modernity

Photographs taken by Western travelers to the Soviet Union in the 1920s and early 1930s offer an independent view of the newly built examples of modern architecture, set against the backdrop of public life in the Soviet capital. Among these travelers was the American glaciologist William Osgood Field (1904–1994), whose photographs are shown on the following pages. During his expeditions to Georgia's glaciers in 1929, 1931 and 1933, he made inevitable stopovers in Moscow, where he documented scenes from the city's everyday life: May Day demonstrations, life at a flea market, children having lunch at school and other moments. In his photographs, which are preserved in the collections of the University of Wisconsin-Milwaukee, two recently completed projects by Konstantin Melnikov are clearly visible: the Kauchuk Club (1927–1929) and the New Sukharev Market (1924–1926). Together, they form a portrait not only of architectural ambition, but of a real city in motion.

May 1st demonstrations near Red Square, Moscow, 1931

1728

Installation of May 1st decorations, Melnikov's Kauchuk Club,
Moscow, 1931

ЕВОЛЮЦИОННЫХ СИЛ МЕЖДУНАРОДНОГО ПРОЛЕТАРИАТА.
5
В
4
завода имени
годовщины 10 октября
БИБЛИОТЕКА-ЧИТАЛЬНЯ ЭНГЕЛЬСА
1059

Melnikov's entrance gates to the New Sukharev Market, with circular supergraphics and a triangular canopy in the background of the unofficial flea market, Moscow, 1929

Children having lunch at a primary school, Moscow, 1933

Robert Maillart's cold storage and warehouse for Gerhard & Hay,
St. Petersburg, 1912

The Swiss Connection

Marianne Burkhalter and Christian Sumi

Eighteenth and Nineteenth Centuries

The Ticino architects Domenico Trezzini, Domenico Gilardi and Antonio Adamini emigrated to Russia in the eighteenth and nineteenth centuries. They became leading architects of the Baroque and Classicist movements in St. Petersburg.

Twentieth Century

Between 1912 and 1918, the Swiss civil engineer Robert Maillart built important infrastructure projects in the former Tsarist Empire – namely, in St. Petersburg, Riga and Kharkiv.

El Lissitzky worked on his Wolkenbügel project together with the architects Emil Roth and Mart Stam during his stay at a health resort in Ticino from 1924 to 1925.

Hannes Meyer was director of the Bauhaus from 1928 to 1930, succeeding Walter Gropius. After his time at the Bauhaus, he moved to the Soviet Union in 1930. His fellow Basel colleague Hans Schmidt, one of the cofounders of the Congrès Internationaux d'Architecture Moderne (CIAM), also moved to Moscow in 1930. Both returned, disappointed, in 1936/1937.

Le Corbusier built the Centrosoyuz in Moscow from 1928 to 1933. He also participated in the competition for the new Palace of Soviets (1931–1932), his entry becoming an icon of European modernism.

Twenty-First Century

The Russian architect Alexander Brodsky, the poet among today's architects in Russia, recently taught at ETH Zurich.

Verena Huber and Eugene Asse – founder of the MARCH architecture school in Moscow – are currently establishing long-term contacts between Switzerland and Russia.

In 2019, burkhalter sumi were invited to contribute to an exhibition and catalog on the Russian engineer Vladimir Shukhov and the German-American designer Konrad Wachsmann.

Bibliography on Konstantin Melnikov

Baldeweg, Juan Navarro, and Andrés Jaque. *Konstantin Melnikov: aparcamiento para 1000 autos. 2a variante. París, 1925*. Madrid: Rueda, 2004.

Barth, Fritz. *Konstantin Melnikov and His House*. Stuttgart and London: Edition Axel Menges, 2015.

Chatwin, Bruce. "Konstantin Melnikov: Architect." *Granta* 26 (Spring 1989): 117–125.

Chepkunova, Irina, Irina Korobina and Pavel Kuznetsov, eds. *Arkhitektor Konstantin Melnikov: Pavilyony, garazhi, kluby i zhilye sovetskoy epokhi* [*Architect Konstantin Melnikov: Pavilions, Garages, Clubs and Houses of the Soviet Era*]. Moscow: Kuchkovo Pole, Schusev State Museum of Architecture, 2015.

Cohen, Jean-Louis. "Il padiglione di Melnikov a Parigi: una seconda ricostruzione." *Casabella* no. 529 (November 1986): 40–51.

Cooke, Catherine. *Russian Avant-Garde: Theories of Art, Architecture and the City*. London: Academy Editions, 1995.

De Magistris, Alessandro. *La casa cilindrica di Konstantin Melnikov: 1927–1929*. Turin: Celid, 1998.

———. "Konstantin Mel'nikov: l'Architetto e il Tempo." *Casabella* no. 839–840 (July–August 2014): 72–91 (English text: 102–105).

———. "Konstantin Mel'nikov: 1925–1930." *Casabella* no. 841 (September 2014), 80–103 (English text: 113–117).

———. "Konstantin Mel'nikov: Gli Anni di Stalin, il Limbo, il Disgelo." *Casabella* no. 843 (November 2014), 4–25 (English text: 120–122).

Fosso, Mario, Otakar Máčel and Maurizio Merrigi, eds. *Konstantin S. Mel'nikov and the Construction of Moscow*. Milan: Skira, 2000.

Garrido, Ginés, ed. *Melnikov*. Madrid: Electa, 2001.

———. *Mélnikov en París, 1925*. Barcelona: Fundación Caja de Arquitectos, 2011.

Gozak, Andrei. *Dom Mel'nikova* [*The Melnikov House*]. Moscow: S. E. Gordeyev, 2010.

Khan-Magomedov, Selim. *Konstantin Mel'nikov* [*Konstantin Melnikov*]. Moscow: Stroyizdat, 1990.

Konstantin Melnikov: Risunki i proekty; Katalog vystavki [*Konstantin Melnikov: Drawings and Projects*]. Exhibition catalog. Moscow: Sovetsky Khudozhnik, 1989.

Kuznetsov, Pavel. *The Melnikov House: Icon of the Avant-Garde, Family Home, Architecture Museum*. Berlin: DOM Publishers, 2017, 2nd edition published in 2021.

Kuznetsov, Pavel, Tapani Mustonen and Tatyana Tsareva, eds. *Melnikov House: Research Report and Recommendations for a Conservation Plan*. Moscow: Schusev State Museum of Architecture and Los Angeles: Getty Foundation, 2019.

Kuznetsov, Pavel, Anna Kistanova and Patricia Semeniuk, eds. *Melnikoff / Мельников*. Exhibition catalog. Moscow: Schusev State Museum of Architecture, 2022.

Kuznetsov, Pavel, and Narine Tyutcheva, eds. *Dom Melnikova: Arkhitekturnoye issledovanie* [*Melnikov House: Architectural Study*]. Yekaterinburg: TATLIN, 2022.

Mullagildin, Rishat, ed. *Konstantin Melnikov: The Architecture, 1920s–1930s*. Tokyo: Toto Shupan, 2002.

Nekrasov, Viktor. "How I Met a Dinosaur and What Happened." *The Times Literary Supplement*, no. 3,811, March 1975.

Pallasmaa, Juhani, and Andrei Gozak. *The Melnikov House: Moscow (1927–1929)*. London: Academy Editions, 1996.

Ranzani, Ermanno. "Mosca 1927: La casa di K.S. Melnikov." *Domus* no. 672 (May 1986): 74–87.

Starr, S. Frederick. *Melnikov: Solo Architect in a Mass Society*. Princeton: Princeton University Press, 1978.

———. *Il padiglione di Melnikov a Parigi: 1925*. Rome: Officina Edizioni, 1979.

Strigalyov, Anatoly, and Irina Kokkinaki, eds. *Konstantin Stepanovich Mel'nikov: Arkhitektura moey zhizni: Tvorcheskaya kontseptsiya. Tvorcheskaya praktika* [*Konstantin Stepanovich Melnikov: The Architecture of My Life: Creative Conception: Creative Practice*]. Moscow: Iskusstvo, 1985.

Wortmann, Arthur, ed. *Melnikov: The Muscles of Invention*. Rotterdam: Van Hezik-Fonds 90, 1990.

Bibliography on the Swiss connection

Bill, Max. *Robert Maillart: Bridges and Constructions*. New York: Frederick A. Praeger Publishers, 1969.

El Lissitzky: Der Traum vom Wolkenbügel: El Lissitzky – Emil Roth – Mart Stam. Zurich: gta Verlag, 1991.

Gisler, Omar. *Terra d'Artisi*. Zurich: AS Verlag, 2022.

Kirikova, Olga. "Robert Maillart in St. Petersburg." *WB+W* (April 2005), 70–72.

Konovaloga, Olga. "Robert Maillart as a Structural Engineer and Entrepreneur in Kharkiv (1915–1918)," Ph.D. dissertation, ETH Zurich, Institute gta, Prof. Dr. Laurent Stalder, Prof. Em. Kees Christiaanse. Zurich, 2029.

Kuznetsov, Pavel. "Architectural Legacy of El Lissitzky: Utopias, Theories and Practice." In *El Lissitzky and Switzerland*, edited by Carole Haensler. Zurich: Scheidegger & Spiess, 2025.

Navone, Nicola, and Letizia Tedeschi, eds. *Dal mito al progetto: La cultura architectonico dei maestri italiani e ticinese nella Russia neoclassica*. Archivio del moderno/Accademia di architettura di Mendrisio/Museo Cantonale. Mendrisio, 2003.

Nozhova, Ekaterina. *Networks of Construction*. Institute of Historic Building Research and Conservation, ETH Zurich. Munich: Hirmer, 2016.

Oechslin, Werner, ed. *Mart Stam: Eine Reise in die Schweiz: 1923–1925*. Zurich: gta Verlag, 1991.

Project International, ed. *Architektura: Sdjelano w Schwejzarii: 10 tem – 10 projektow / Architektur: Hergestellt in der Schweiz: 10 Themen – 10 Projekte*. Moscow, 2002.

Schnaidt, Claude, and Hannes Meyer. *Bauten, Projekte und Schriften*. Teufen: Niggli, 1965.

Schmidt, Hans, Mart Stam, El Lissitzky and Emil Roth, eds. *ABC. Beiträge zum Bauen, 1924–1928*. Zurich: Lars Müller Publishers, 1993.

Sumi, Christian. "Konrad Wachsmann – Pioneer of Industrial Construction." In *Shukhov: Formula of Architecture*. Moscow, 2019.

Suter, Ursula, ed. *Hans Schmidt (1893–1972): Architekt in Basel, Moskau, Berlin Ost*. Zurich: gta Verlag, 1993.

Konstantin Melnikov at the groundbreaking ceremony
for the Kauchuk Club in Moscow, November 6, 1927

I am accused of being pretentious, of indulging in fantasy and utopianism. Yet the dreamer Melnikov built dozens of real standing buildings.

Меня обвиняют в оригальничаньи, в фантастике и утопичности моих проектов. Между тем, фантаст Мельников построил десятки реально стоящих сооружений.

K. M., 1935

Biography

How It All Began

1890
Konstantin Melnikov is born in a peasant family in a village near Moscow, Russia

1903
Meets Vladimir Chaplin, an engineer, inventor, businessman and philanthropist

1905–1917
Studies at the Moscow School of Painting, Sculpture and Architecture

1912
Marries Anna Yablokova (Lyudmila is born in 1913, Viktor in 1914)

1914–1918
World War I

1917–1920
Revolution and Civil War in Russia

1917–1920
First steps in architecture: facades for AMO automobile factory, village for the staff of the Alekseyevskaya Psychiatric Hospital, workers' settlements, first sketches for his own house

How to Become an Avant-Gardist

1918–1922
Designs "New Moscow" city plan in architecture studio under the Moscow City Council, led by Ivan Zholtovsky and Alexey Schusev

1922–1924
Teaches in "New Academy" studio (VKhUTEMAS School) with Ilya Golosov

1921–1928
New Economic Policy

1922–1923
First avant-garde designs: Palace of Labor,* "Saw" housing estate,* Makhorka exhibition pavilion

1924
Building up reputation: sarcophagus for Lenin's body, Arcos building,* Leningrad Pravda building,* New Sukharev Market, USSR pavilion for Paris exposition

Golden Age

1925
Year in France: USSR pavilion and trade sector kiosks, and garages for Paris; cold reception upon return to Moscow

1926
Crematorium,* pavilion in Thessaloníki, catafalque for Leonid Krasin

1926–1928
Bus and truck garages for the City of Moscow

1927–1929
Building his own house-studio

1927–1930
Workers' clubs: out of seven designs, six are built

International exhibitions: Warsaw (1926), New York (1927), Milan (1933)

1928–1929
Early projects for Park of Culture and Leisure

Competition projects: Columbus* (Santo Domingo, 1929), Green City* (1930), MOSPS Theater* (1930–1931), Frunze military academy* (1931), Park of Culture and Leisure* (1931)

1931
Arbat Square reconstruction project

End of Career – Hard Times – Rehabilitation

1932
Stalin's cultural revolution, Union of Soviet Architects, socialist realism

1932–1933
Palace of Labor (Tashkent) and Palace of Nations*

1933
Appointed head of the Moscow City Council's Architectural Studio No. 7

1934–1936
NKTP building,* Moscow River embankments, Izvestia housing, Intourist and Gosplan garages

1935
Second trip to Paris: 1937 USSR exhibition pavilion*

1936–1937
Campaign against Melnikov; dismissal from professorship at the Architecture Institute

1938
Banned from practicing architecture

1938–1964
Years of oblivion and survival

1941–1945
Soviet Union in World War II

1949–1974
Teaching at second-rate educational institutions

1965–1974
Late rehabilitation and return to public life

Final competition projects: USSR pavilion in New York* (1962) and children's cinema* (1967)

1960s
Work on autobiographical manuscript, *Architecture of My Life*

1974
Passes away

1978
First book about him is published by Frederick S. Starr

*competition entry

Unless otherwise indicated, all projects are for Moscow and Moscow Region.

Image Credits

t = top
m = middle
b = bottom
l = left
r = right

cover, 16–18, 20–22, 24–26, 28–29, 30(t), 32–34, 36–38, 42, 43(b), 44, 54–56, 60(t), 74, 80–81(t), 82(b), 83–86, 90–92, 129(r): Alberto Canepa

8, 10–11, 12(b), 13(b), 14–15, 40–41, 46–49, 52–53, 58–59, 60(b), 62–64, 66–68, 70–72, 78–79, 88, 96–97, 98(b), 99(b), 100–102, 103(t), 104–105, 109(t, m), 110–111, 122–123(b), 124–125, 127(t), 129(l), 130, 131(t) : Vladislav Ogay

9: Emanuele Cipolla, Massimo Contini

12(t)–13(t): Simone Mirabella, Nora Soldati

19(l): source: *Blok*, no. 11 (March 1926), 25–26.

19(r): source: *Vechernyaya Moscow* [Evening Moscow], no. 227 (October 1924).

23(t), 144–151: from the American Geographical Society Library, University of Wisconsin-Milwaukee Libraries

23(b), 30(b), 31, 73, 75, 80–81(b), 82(t), 126, 127(b): Fabrizio Rocchè

27: source: *France et Russie*, no. 2 (March 1925), 26.

35: source: Konstantin Melnikov, "Oformlenie projekta" [Project Design], *USSR Architecture*, no. 5 (1933): 35.

39: source: Frederick S. Starr, *Melnikov: Solo Architect in a Mass Society* (Princeton: Princeton University Press, 1978), 104.

43(t), 45: source: V. S. Sokov, *Garages: Basics of the Design of Automotive Maintenance Buildings* (Leningrad: State Publishing House for Transport Literature, 1935), 12–13.

50–51: source: Nikolay Lukhmanov, *Cylindrichesky dom* [Cylindrical House], *Stroitelstvo Moskvy* [Construction of Moscow], no. 5 (May 1929), 16–18.

57: source: Nikolay Lukhmanov, *Architektura kluba* [Architecture of Clubs] (Moscow, 1930), 70–71.

61: source: "Klub kommunalnikov na Stromynke" [Club of Communal Union on Stromynka street], *Stroitelstvo Moskvy* [Construction of Moscow], no. 11 (November 1927), 5.

65(t): source: Nikolay Lukhmanov, *Architektura kluba* [Architecture of Clubs] (Moscow, 1930), 60–61.

65(b): source: "Novye kluby u khimikov" [New Clubs of Chemical Industry Union], *Stroitelstvo Moskvy* [Construction of Moscow], no. 1 (January 1928), 18.

69: source: Michel Ilyine, "L'architecture du Club Ouvrier en U.R.S.S.," *l'Architecture d'Aujourd'hui*, no. 8 (November 1931), 18.

76–77: source: Konstantin Melnikov, "Gorod ratsionalisirovannogo otdykha" [A City of Rationalized Recreation], *Stroitelstvo Moskvy* [Construction of Moscow], no. 3 (March 1930), 21.

87: source: A. Karra, "*Arkhitektura teatra*" [Architecture of Theater], *Stroitelstvo Moskvy* [Construction of Moscow], no. 7 (July 1932), 16.

89: source: M. Minkus and Shass Yu, "Proektirovaniye Krasnoznamennoy Voennoy Akademii RKKA imeni M.V. Frunze" [Design of Frunze Military Academy], *Sovetskaya Architektura* [Soviet Architecture], no. 5 (May 1933), 37.

93: Mara Mari, Francisco Silva

98(t), 99(t): Inaya Berger, Hadiseh Karimi

103(b): Sveva Bonapace, Maura Pagani

106: Ada Fortunati, Cristina Meregalli

107: source: Yakov Kornfeld, "Projects of Soviet Pavilion for Paris International Exposition 1937," *Arkhitekturnaya Gazeta* [Architecture Newspaper], annex to no. 33 (1936), 4.

109(b): Kyrre Beck Myreng, Lucia Prieto Heras

122(t), 123(t): source: I. Leonidov, *Lenin Institute*: *Sovremennaya Architectura* [Contemporary Architecture]. no. 4–5 (April–May 1927), 120, 123.

128: source: *Architetti Russi per Cristoforo Colombo: Santo Domingo 1929* (Brescia: Edizioni Nuovi Strumenti, 1993), 42.

133–140: El Lissitzky and N. A. Ladovsky (eds.), *Izvestiya ASNOVA* [ASNOVA Bulletin], (Moscow, June 1926), Yale University Library, New Haven, USA.

152: source: Max Bill, *Robert Maillart: Bridges and Constructions* (New York: Frederick A. Praeger Publishers, 1969), 167.

156: source: unknown author, The Russian State Documentary Film and Photo Archive, Krasnogorsk, Russia, inv. 15412, *Groundbreaking Ceremony for the Kauchuk Club* (November 1929).

We have made every effort to identify all rights holders. Should despite our intensive research any person entitled to rights have been overlooked, they are kindly asked to contact the publisher.

About the Editors

Pavel Kuznetsov (*1971) is a researcher of twentieth-century architecture, museologist and curator. From 2022 to 2024, he was a lecturer on the Soviet avant-garde at the Accademia di architettura di Mendrisio, Switzerland. Since 2024, he has been a visiting researcher at the University of Kassel, Germany. He served as first deputy director of the Schusev State Museum of Architecture in Moscow (2010–2022) and was the founding director of the State Melnikovs Museum (2014–2022).

He oversaw the collections and archives of the Melnikov House and its transition from a private home to a public museum. He also led the pre-conservation survey of the house (2017–2019), supported by the Getty Foundation, and is the author of *The Melnikov House: Icon of the Avant-Garde, Family Home, Architecture Museum* (Berlin: DOM Publishers, 2017, 2nd edition: 2021).

He curated the exhibitions *Melnikov / Le Corbusier: rencontre à la villa Savoye* (2017, Villa Savoye, Paris); *Melnikoff / Мельников* (2022, Schusev State Museum of Architecture, Moscow); and *Melnikov: Architect of the Impossible* (2023) and *Soviet Architectural Avant-Garde: Utopias, Theories and Practice* (2024), both at the Accademia di architettura di Mendrisio.

Marianne Burkhalter (*1947) completed an apprenticeship as an architectural draftswoman, worked as an architect in Florence (Superstudio), New York and Los Angeles (Studio Works) and was a visiting student at Princeton University. She has taught at the Southern California Institute of Architecture (SCI-ARC) in Los Angeles and at Lausanne's federal institute of technology, the École Polytechnique Fédérale de Lausanne (EPFL).

Christian Sumi (*1950) studied at ETH Zurich, where he worked for the Institut für Geschichte und Theorie der Architektur (Institute for the History and Theory of Architecture) (gta). He has taught at the Harvard Graduate School of Design, at EPFL Lausanne and at the University of Strathclyde in Glasgow. Christian Sumi is the author of *The Goddess – La Déesse: Investigations on the Legendary Citroën DS*, published by Lars Müller Publishers in 2020.

Marianne Burkhalter and Christian Sumi founded burkhalter sumi architekten in 1984. The firm has built up an international reputation, inter alia for its innovative wooden architecture and distinctive polychrome palette. From 2008 to 2016, they held a joint full professorship at the Accademia di architettura di Mendrisio, and they founded their own studio in 2020. Marianne Burkhalter and Christian Sumi were awarded the Prix Meret Oppenheim in 2024.

Acknowledgments

For their generous support, which made this publication possible, we thank
Andrea et Darya Bassi architectes, Geneva;
Christ & Gantenbein, Basel, Barcelona;
E2A Piet Eckert Wim Eckert Architekten, Zurich, Berlin, Warsaw;
Graber Pulver Architekt:innen, Zurich, Bern;
Meili, Peter & Partner Architekten, Zurich.

We would like to thank the Accademia di architettura di Mendrisio – and especially its director, Walter Angonese, the dean's office coordinator, Marco della Torre; and Professor Christoph Frank – for for the inclusion of courses on the Soviet architectural avant-garde in the Accademia's curriculum, and for generously providing the models that form the foundation of this publication. Our gratitude also goes to the Accademia's exhibition coordinator, Stefania Murer, and photographer, Alberto Canepa.

We thank all participants of the courses on Melnikov at the Accademia di architettura for their sincere and enthusiastic interest in the history of early Soviet modernism.

We further thank the Architekturforum Zürich for their support in organizing the exhibition accompanying this book.

Our thanks also go to Lars Müller and his team at Lars Müller Publishers, in particular Rebekka Seiz and Emilia Maier, for their support and collaboration.

We thank Fabrizio Rocchè, who significantly helped with presenting Melnikov's architectural drawings.

Last but not least, Pavel Kuznetsov is grateful to his partner, Vladislav Ogay, who supported his research and teaching on Konstantin Melnikov in every possible way and substantially contributed to the visual and scenographic presentation of Melnikov's legacy to the public.

Melnikov
An Investigation Through Architectural Models

Editors: Pavel Kuznetsov, Marianne Burkhalter, Christian Sumi
Texts: Pavel Kuznetsov
Translation of texts by Melnikov: Pavel Kuznetsov
Translation of text by Ladovsky: Elisaveta Kriman
Copyediting and proofreading: Rita Forbes
Project coordination: Emilia Maier
Design: Lars Müller Publishers / Lars Müller with Rebekka Seiz
Production: Rebekka Seiz
Lithography: Gundula Seraphin, Bad Münstereifel, Germany
Printing and binding: Printer Trento s.r.l., Trento, Italy
Paper: Munken Lynx, 130 g/m^2

Lars Müller Publishers is supported by the Swiss Federal Office of Culture with a structural contribution for the years 2021–2025.

Lars Müller Publishers
Pfingstweidstrasse 6
8005 Zurich, Switzerland
+41 44 274 37 40
info@lars-mueller-publishers.com
www.lars-mueller-publishers.com

Product safety
Producer: Lars Müller Publishers GmbH
Responsible person in accordance with EU Regulation 2023/988 (GPSR): Michael Klein, sales representative, Hub 1, DE-84149 Velden
+49 8742 964 552 2, gpsr@lars-mueller-publishers.com

ISBN 978-3-03778-803-5

Distributed in North America, Latin America and the Caribbean by ARTBOOK | D.A.P.
www.artbook.com

Printed in Italy

This publication is being released to accompany the exhibition at the Architekturforum Zürich in fall 2025.

ARCHITEKTURFORUM ZÜRICH